Change Your Mind

D1416306

CHANGE YOUR MIND *Life*

Teri D. Mahaney, Ph.D.

Supertraining Press

CHANGE YOUR MIND
Copyright © 1989 by Teri D. Mahaney

The author freely grants permission to quote up to 350 words of this text as long as proper credit is given. She encourages readers to distribute copies of the scripts to friends for their personal use. However, use of these scripts for commercial purposes will require a royalty agreement.

First Edition: 1989
Revised Edition: 1991

Cover design by Harriet Drummund, Anchorage, Alaska
and Robert Howard, Fort Collins, Colorado

Published in the United States by
Supertraining Press
133 East de la Guerra, Suite 409
Santa Barbara, California 93101
(800) 762-9937

Mahaney, Teri D.
    Change your mind,life/ Teri Mahaney – Santa Barbara, CA:
Supertraining Press, c1989
        254 p.:port.; 23 cm.
        On t.p. "life" is written across "mind".
        Includes bibliographical references.
        ISBN 0-9624140-1-8
1. Subliminal perception. 2. Audiotapes in psychology. 3. Success – Audio-visual aids. 4. Success – Psychological aspects. 5. Affirmations. I. Title II. Title: Change your mind. III. Title: Change your life.
BF323.S8M34 1989   **153.7'36– dc20**   **89–51990**
                                                                    AACR 2 MARC

Library of Congress

For the women and men
who helped me create this program

Table of Contents

Clearing and Completing
Confidentiality
Consciousness
Control
Decision Making and Problem Solving
Financial Planning
Focusing
Global Community
Goal Setting
Healing: Christian
Health and Healing: General
Holograms and Synergy
Integrity and Ethics
Performing Well
Personal Power
Prosperity: Personal I
Prosperity: Personal II
Receiving and Being Supported
Relationships
Relationships: Intimacy
Releasing and Forgiving
Sales Calls and Cold Calling
Self Esteem
Speaking: Public
Spirituality
Success I
Success I: Female
Success I: Male
Success II: Ambition
Success II: Business
Test Taking
Time Management
Transcendence
Winning Friends and Influencing People
Wrestling
Writing

Order Forms

The Creation of Change Your Mind:

The Program Beginnings
and the People Who Made it Work

I've always been curious about people who *make it* and people who don't. I probably wasn't supposed to *make it*, but I did, and I always wondered why. I was a bright teen who questioned authority and only followed rules that made sense to me. Consequently, I got kicked out of one high school and two colleges. Each "disciplinary action" was for the same reason — not living where the school administrators wanted me to, like a particular district or a particular dormitory. Of course, the same rules I was punished for breaking were changed a short time later, which made me even more determined to do it my way! I was a stubborn independent thinker living by my own rules. I was self validating and believed in learning and experiencing. I was destined to struggle.

Characterized as a Type A over-achiever, I went on to earn a Ph.D. and a six-figure income. Along the way, I alternated focusing on my career, raising a fine young daughter on my own, travelling abroad, rafting 1000 miles of white water rivers, living in Alaska, and enjoying close relationships with many wonderful friends. I read voluminously, averaging 100 books a year, and sampled many groups, schools, and movements. While studying with the Association of Research and Enlightenment, I analyzed my dreams, discovered my soul's purpose, used castor oil packs, and focused on "mind is the builder." I read Ram Dass and concentrated on being here now. I read Shakti Gawain and scotch-taped affirmations to my bathroom mirror and created treasure maps. I meditated, fasted, and cleansed. Each experience helped me and my life improved. But I continued to struggle.

I struggled with jobs — so I formed my own businesses, ultimately becoming a consultant. I struggled with relationships — and discovered true intimacy and feminism. I struggled with my daughter's dyslexia which created years of frustration for both of us — and moved into brain research, hypnosis, and acupuncture. I struggled with my own development, and got into past-llife regressions, rolfing, reiki, and releasing what didn't work. Each step felt better, so I kept going. *Where, I didn't know.*

Life is What Happens When You're Making Other Plans
(Betty Talmadge, American meat broker, b. 1924)

I never intended to make my own supraliminal (or subliminal) tapes, much less help other people make theirs. It all happened coincidentally (if you believe in coincidences).

I was teaching business courses for the community college in Anchorage, Alaska, and developing *Supertraining*, a management consulting and training company. I specialized in developing new courses, new topics, new perspectives, new materials. Denis Waitley's Psychology of Winning (POW) program was new, so of course, I wanted to take it. The college personnel director liked the idea and flew up a POW trainer to present the course to college teachers. I took the course and began teaching it myself.

Via video, Waitley introduced me to the accelerated learning research. He suggested changing my self image using these same techniques, which was "new" to me. I read *Superlearning©* which explained the accelerated learning process developed by Georgi Lozanov in Bulgaria. Intrigued, I attended the Lozanov Institute's five-day training program and was certified in his Suggestopedia method. I quickly incorporated these accelerated learning techniques into my college teaching and business training and I began experimenting with music, music therapy, and listening therapy.

The *Change Your Mind* program developed as I put it all together — combining self help with Suggestopedia. I wrote a positive affirmation script on goal setting, time management, and delegation (the self help part) and recorded the script on an audio tape with a background of baroque music, repeating each affirmation three times to an eight-second cadence (the Suggestopedia part).

Skeptical but curious, I began listening to the tape each afternoon in a relaxed state. But it didn't work. The tape automatically put me to sleep. After listening to the tape for three consecutive days and falling asleep each day, I threw the tape away, sure I had wasted my time. Ten days later, I realized the tape was working! In ten days, I had organized my office, delegated two major projects which had been on hold for a year, and written long term goals. Intrigued, I began studying subliminals and learned about supraliminals.

My account of this incident interested my friends, who experimented with the system. They sent friends, who sent friends. I began charging a fee for consulting and helped clients write their own personal scripts. At this stage, everything was experimental, and every script was completely individualized and unique. The tapes worked, and the word spread. More people came, and I raised my fees.

Some standard themes came up repeatedly such as self esteem and change, and many people requested scripts for particular issues like test taking and goal setting. I developed standardized scripts and prepared information on how they worked. Each client became a co-creator of the program in some way, contributing a new question or insight or reaction that helped me modify a script or change a procedure. *My clients taught me as we went!*

Throughout this process, I studied subliminal research and talked with subliminal tape producers. I found the research to be mainly technical and argumentative; it didn't deal with behavior change (except for Silverman's work: see Chapter Six). And tape producers didn't get long term follow-up and feedback from their clients as I did, so it was difficult for them to know what really worked and what didn't.

For instance, I quickly learned that subliminal tapes made with a male voice didn't work for many women. Abused women often became angry listening to a subliminal male voice, even though they couldn't hear it consciously. Conversely, all men I worked with accepted the female voice in their subconscious. Yet most of the commercial subliminal tapes were being made with a male voice, limiting their effectiveness.

I began questioning the effectiveness of commercial tapes, and I subsequently recorded a few commercial scripts using the *Change Your Mind* system. Many not only didn't work but actually created or intensified the condition they were designed to eliminate.

I became more aware of the responsibility involved in making tapes which "program" minds. I wrote a script to program my mind to use the *Change Your Mind* technology in appropriate ways and to write scripts for people which promoted their highest good at all times. I tried new scripts on myself and a group of willing guinea pig friends, and we compared our processes and outcomes. I constantly modified scripts and techniques.

The most difficult scripts for me were on success and money. One year, I made a tape telling my mind to make more money, and it worked. I watched like a bystander while my consulting business grew and my *gross* income *doubled*. At year's end, I was startled and disappointed to discover I had worked harder than ever to earn less *net* income, despite the impressive *gross* figures. I had made more money, but I had kept less. I shifted approaches and worked with prosperity scripts. Then I shifted approaches again and again until I got the success series. I recorded the female success script and *changed my mind* about success, money, ambition, and prosperity. And I wrote the first edition of this book within 90 days after listening to that tape!

While the *Change Your Mind* process was developing, I personally worked with over 400 people. During that period, I grappled with some unsolved problems, saw some wonderful successes, had some great personal breakthroughs, and shared in a few miracles. I had the honor of working with people with courageous pioneer spirits who were willing to experiment with my unproven program and with their own mind/brains. They spent hours writing and recording scripts and providing feedback on what was working and what wasn't. We worked together trying new ideas to create, change, modify, and improve this system for you.

The stories and examples throughout this book represent just a few of those people, and they are real stories about real people.

4

I worked with each of them, and I learned from each of them. Only the names have been changed; the facts are accurate.

Roger tried the *Change Your Mind* program because he was always hitting his head. He felt like a bumbler. He couldn't remember when it all started, but he said it felt like forever. Under self hypnosis, Roger saw himself in a car wreck seven years before, crashing into the windshield. His wife came to the emergency room, looked down at his glass-encrusted head and said, "That's just like Roger to hit his head." Evidently, in his state of shock, her comment served as a sort of hypnotic command which started him hitting his head. We wrote his script to stop hitting his head and included some general statements like *My head is now completely healed* .

When I saw him ten days later, his head had fresh marks on it, but he insisted he hadn't hit his head since listening to his tape. I was wondering if the tape had tricked him into believing he wasn't hitting his head when he actually was. Then he told me the reason for the marks on his head: particles of glass had been working their way out the top of his head for a week. His doctor said it was glass from his accident seven years before, and there was no medical explanation why it was happening now. Roger wondered if the tape could have anything to do with it. Once I recovered from my surprise, I told him what I have told hundreds of people since then: "I don't know, but anything is possible." *From Roger, I learned anything **is** possible, and as a result, I've been willing to work with anyone on any issue, whether or not I thought it was possible.*

Joan tried the *Change Your Mind* program to lose weight. We created a script one afternoon, including eating slowly, chewing thoroughly, and enjoying each meal as a banquet. She listened to her tape one night, and the next day, as she was hurriedly fixing a low calorie frozen dinner for quick eating, something told her to set the table, eat slowly, and enjoy it. Though she was in a hurry, she ate her meal in a leisurely and enjoyable way. I had told her the tapes took three days to work, but she had only listened to her tape once. *From Joan, I learned the system really belongs to the person using it and not to me. I learned not to predict what would happen or how long a process might take, but rather to let my clients teach me what worked and in what amount of time. I also learned how fast this program can work.*

Harry and Nan tried the *Change Your Mind* program because they were given a session as a gift. Harry was a handyman with his own remodeling business, and his wife, Nan, kept the books. A depressed economy was destroying all they had spent a lifetime building, and their self confidence and health were beginning to fail along with their business. They were both skeptical about the program but were willing to listen and try it. Nan started with the *Self Esteem* and *Personal Power* scripts, and Harry started with *Health* and *Success: Male.* Within 60 days, Harry had stopped smoking, changed his eating habits, started taking supplements, and lost 20 pounds. Nan was doing equally well. Both completely changed their lives and felt back in control. They made hard decisions about their finances and started over, building from scratch. *From Harry and Nan, I experienced the power of having support during tough times. They made changes quickly in positive ways, supporting each other throughout the process. I wrote the Receiving/Being Supported script to help others develop that kind of support.*

John tried the *Change Your Mind* program to improve his wrestling team. An experienced coach, John was creating a new college team. Together, we developed a wrestling script (see Chapter Nine), and several of his key players listened to it along with the *Self Esteem* script. Even though the team became #2 in the nation and John got the coach of the year award, the results from the tapes weren't consistent. One of the wrestlers found the tapes worked better for his grade-point average than for his wrestling-point average. Another player was on a winning streak all season and then gave up in the final qualification meet. In subsequent years, however, the wrestling script was tried again. On two separate occasions, mothers of high school wrestlers recorded tapes for their sons. Both wrestlers won the state championship. *From this, I learned the power of the mother's voice. I also learned sports performance is altered by mental programming, but personal and family patterns can sabotage success. I spent two years working on the success scripts and three years designing the clearing script to dissolve those elements of self-sabotage.*

Gladys tried the *Change Your Mind* program for her telephone addiction. She stayed on the phone for so many hours each day that she didn't get anything done. She had purchased a very expensive set of subliminal tapes which didn't help and actually seemed to be making the problem worse. We created a simple script which stated *I talk on the phone at the appropriate times. I talk on the phone for the appropriate length of time, etc.* I never heard from Gladys again, but Sue, her best friend, came in the next month. Sue had seen the change in Gladys and still couldn't believe it, so Sue wanted to try the program. Sue told me Gladys felt she hadn't changed at all and argued with her friends that she was exactly the same way she had always been. *From Gladys, I learned how the power of this program compared with commercial programs. From Gladys and Sue, I learned about the role of denial in the change process, and that others often see the changes we make before we recognize and accept them ourselves.*

Greg tried the *Change Your Mind* program to develop better social skills. He traveled weekly and wanted to meet people more easily. He was quiet and shy and sat scrunched down in his seat, never making eye contact as we worked. We wrote an assertiveness script, including affirmations about meeting people easily, being interesting, and being a good conversationalist. A month later, when we met to discuss his next script, he sat erect and spoke clearly and directly, making eye contact the entire time. He told me of his displeasure about the script we had written, because he had never needed those things. He had always been an interesting man and a good conversationalist. What he needed was self esteem. *From Greg, I learned how totally our self images and actions can change with no conscious recall of what we were before, and how quickly and easily that can happen.*

Diane tried the *Change Your Mind* program because she wasn't getting along with her supervisor, and she wasn't being promoted. She had great vocational skills and was very creative in writing grants to generate millions of dollars, yet she was being moved down in the ranks of her organization. She was also steadily gaining weight. We worked on a script for all those issues except the weight, and included the *Self Esteem* and *Receiving/Being Supported* scripts. Six months later, she left her job to set up her own grant writing and consulting business. She realized she had been sabotaging her own career because she resented financially supporting her husband. By clearing that issue, she lost 30+ pounds and felt great. *From Diane, I learned* *the issues we think we are working on are rarely the real issues, and consequently, many seemingly unrelated problems will dissolve when a major issue is cleared. I also learned to start with the clearing script for weight loss programs.*

Peter tried the *Change Your Mind* program for test taking anxiety. He wanted to be an air traffic controller but failed the test the first time around. Together, we wrote a script on the FAA exam, and I developed the *Test Taking* script (see Chapter Nine). We discussed his father's expectations of him and did some affirmations about Peter being at peace with his father and living his life his own way (I didn't have the *Success:Male* script then). He passed his next exam in the highest percentile and was invited to attend the FAA school in Oklahoma. He declined the invitation, however, after realizing he had chosen that secure career to please his father, not himself. For himself, he chose his artistic love, video production, and within two years, he had developed a fully equipped video studio and a comfortable though modest income. *From Peter, I learned how powerful a parent's scripting can be in our important decisions, and how easy it is to reverse that scripting and gain control of our own lives.*

Bob tried the *Change Your Mind* program because he wanted to go back to school. Bob was in his mid-40's, ready for a career change. He had been a policeman and was working as a state investigator, but he really wanted to be a counselor for troubled youth. For that career, he needed a Master's degree, but he was afraid he wouldn't be able to write the papers required or pass the tests at the graduate level. Twenty years earlier, he had barely made it through undergraduate school. We developed a personalized script for him, and he used the *Self Esteem, Success: Male and Test Taking* scripts. One year later, he graduated with a double Master's degree and was applying for counselor's positions. *From Bob, I learned fear, not ability, is the major block to success, and I began dealing with the underlying causes of fear.*

Suzanne tried the *Change Your Mind* program because she was tired of fighting with everyone. She was a successful real estate agent, but her personal life just wasn't working. She was fighting with her ex-husband, her teenage son, and her boss. She used a clearing script with the *Success: Female* script, which I had just finished. She became very angry, and three days later, she went into her boss' office and yelled at him, demanding he pay her the money he owed her. She was surprised at her behavior, but glad she stood up for herself. Within 90 days, she had re-evaluated her life and her goals and quit her job. She took a year off to enjoy herself and her teenage children. *From Suzanne, I learned that anger is often a healthy part of the change process, and that it's a normal part of the success scripts. I began to see it as a good sign.*

Robert tried the *Change Your Mind* program for stress management for his multiple sclerosis. He had five years to retirement in a top executive position for a national firm and was afraid he wouldn't last. He was experiencing blurred vision and migraines at work. We created a script for his tiredness, blurred vision, and tension, as well as his performance until retirement. And we tried a script for MS, telling his body *to carry the electrical impulses down his spinal cord in rhythmic ways, natural ways, healthy ways, etc.* Six months later, he was vibrant and full of energy and enthusiasm. His MS appeared unchanged, but the tension and migraines were gone. He was busy making his retirement plans, stress free. *From Robert, I began to learn the difference between structural disease which doesn't appear to respond to subliminal suggestion, and the mind/brain issues that do respond to the program.*

Linda tried the *Change Your Mind* program for stress management for her chemotherapy. She had undergone surgery to remove a cancerous ovary and was in chemo treatments every ten days. She was a doctor herself and didn't really believe in subliminals, but she was desperate and willing to try anything. Her chemotherapy was debilitating. She had several days of illness after each treatment, about one or two days of ease, and then several days of anxiety before the next treatment. Because of that pattern, she was unable to work, and her clinic was facing severe financial trouble. We wrote a clearing script for chemotherapy (see Chapter Three) and added affirmations like *I am at peace with my chemotherapy. I flow with my chemotherapy treatments. My body handles my chemotherapy treatments with ease. My body handles my chemotherapy treatments in peace.* She was losing her hair, so we added *My hair is thick and luxurious, etc.* She recorded her tape and called me back after one night of listening to report it worked. She told me she had tried very hard to work up anxiety about her next chemo treatment, telling herself how terrible it would be, but she didn't generate any stress. She was surprised by the success of the tape, and I was touched by her openness. She continued to lose her hair, however, until the chemo treatments stopped. The last time I saw her, she was happy, healthy, and busy in her clinic. *From Linda, I learned the program works for stress reduction (whether or not you believe in it).*

Kevin tried the *Change Your Mind* program for his cerebral palsy (CP). He was convinced the tapes would cure him: I wasn't. We wrote a physiological script and added a clearing script for CP. I added *I am at peace with CP, I embrace CP.* He became angry just hearing the words and didn't want to say them, much less record them, but he did. When he started sleeping to the tape, he had two days of intense anger. He called me each morning and reported, "Doc, I'm chewing nails and just waiting for someone to come by so I can pick a fight." Within three days, the changes started. He had a soft drink addiction and kept two refrigerators fully stocked with cases of cokes. He sold one of the refrigerators and began maintaining a normal week long supply of soft drinks. His physical appearance improved, and he transferred to a new location with his job. His CP symptoms weren't changing, but he was doing well and had begun to see himself talking to large groups of people, perhaps as a national speaker. *From Kevin, I learned that reversing the physical symptoms may not be as important as having the courage to try. While he didn't get what he wanted — a miracle healing — he did get purpose and self esteem.*

And of course, I've personally tried **Change Your Mind** for all aspects of my life, using most of the scripts in this book and many personalized ones for specific situations. I use **Change Your Mind** when I'm feeling blocked or in conflict or just to experiment with a new topic. I've dissolved blocks and released conflict to its highest good and most appropriate outcomes. I've made as many as two tapes in one month, and as few as three in one year. The script writing process itself has become a natural and enjoyable part of my self exploration and problem solving.

What has worked best for me? Among the prepared scripts, the best were *Personal Power, Receiving/Being Supported, Global Consciousness*, and *Success: Female* as I expected.

But I'm often surprised. I once recorded the *Clearing Grieving* script for a friend who had lost a loved one. I made a copy for myself just to experiment. After listening two nights, I became very angry about a personal relationship and made major changes in it. Though I don't know the connection between my friend's tape and that relationship (most likely, it was the section on transcending denial), I'm delighted with the effect!

For transformational change, the clearing scripts have been the most effective (see Chapter Three). My personal patterns changed completely when I cleared my childhood programming of *being a good girl* and *putting myself first.* I made an easy mid-life career transition by clearing *financial security, keeping commitments*, and *staying to get the job done right*, which were my family issues. I maintained calm and peace throughout a deposition after I cleared the *legal system and attorneys.* (Copies of these scripts are in Chapter Three.)

Overall, my most important tape has been the clearing script on struggle. Since making that tape, I have continued to release struggle on every level of my life. I live in harmony most of the time, despite life's challenges. I'm doing what I want to do, and I'm being who I want to be.

It has been a great adventure to develop this program, use it myself, and share it with others. And working with **Change Your Mind** has changed my mind. I now expect everybody to make it, in one way or another. Each of us is unique, and each of us can have a life of purpose and joy, in our own way.

Change Your Mind was developed for you. In some ways, it's like other systems; it deals with self limiting beliefs. But in many ways, it's very different. The program combines Suggestopedia research with subliminal research and blends them with traditional and non-traditional approaches to self help, psychology, and healing.

But the most important difference is you. You make the program different when you become a working partner with your own subconscious mind. You make the program different with your self exploration and experimentation. By taking the time and energy to create your own personal scripts and tapes, you direct your change, growth, and healing.

Change Your Mind was designed for you.
Personalize it, change it, and make it yours.

I wish you the best,

and I know you will *change your life*,

when you.... ***Change Your Mind***.

2

Using Affirmations in Your Scripts

You can change your mind about anything — it's as easy as asking and receiving. We so rarely ask, and we're so hesitant to receive. **Change Your Mind** (CYM) is a way of asking for what you want and being open to receive it.

With the CYM system, you ask for what you want by writing a script, recording it onto a tape in your voice, and "listening" to it at night while you sleep. Your script locks in at your deepest levels and creates permanent changes in your mind and life, easily and effortlessly.

You ask for what you want with affirmations. Affirmations are positive statements that **affirm** in your mind what you want to be or have or do, which may be dramatically different from what is happening in your life now. For instance, you might be alone and feeling lonely but desiring a loving, fulfilling relationship. By **affirming** you are in that relationship now and planting that message in your mind/brain during sleep (the theta brain-wave state), you direct your brain to begin creating the conditions that create that relationship for you.

Often, affirmations conflict with your "self talk" and are hard to accept. Self talk is what you say to yourself — your internal dialogue, your mental conversation. Self talk thoughts, images, and feelings float through your mind/brain continually — about 50,000 a day — and most of them are negative: *I can't; I don't have enough time; It'll never work; I can't afford it.* Affirmations reverse those negative self talk statements to positive self talk: *I can; I have all the time I need to do everything I want; It works perfectly for me and for my highest good now; My income now exceeds my expenses.*

The more difficult the positive affirmations are to believe, the more you probably need them! I started using affirmations in 1976 and experienced exciting results with them, but sometimes they worked and sometimes they didn't. I didn't understand the inconsistent results until I realized some messages were buried so deeply in my brain that they had to be removed equally deeply. The CYM system works on those deepest levels, dissolving negative and limiting self talk at its origins.

The CYM system is a simple way to revise your past, re-invent yourself, and create a new future. It is a process which grows with you and changes with you, working on every level — mental, physical, emotional, and spiritual. With CYM, you dissolve old self talk/mental patterning and replace it with positive possibility thinking, doing, and being. The system can be used at any stage of your process. I've used CYM for years, and I'm still learning to expand my affirmations — to expand what I ask for and what I am willing to receive — and to have the courage to ask to have it all!

Consider starting your CYM program with a customized tape on self esteem and change. Changing your mind about who you really are and about how you handle change provides a good foundation for your future work with your tapes.

How to Use the Prepared Scripts

Prepared affirmation scripts appear in Chapter Nine by subject. Choose a subject that interests you, such as *Self Esteem,* and read through that script with a pen in your hand. Make notes onto the script, changing sentences or words to fit your personal style and vocabulary. Personalize the scripts as much as possible.

Be aware of your "self talk" as you read each sentence/affirmation. Your self talk about each sentence/affirmation in your script is important because the affirmations you agree with have

14

the *least* value for you. Conversely, the affirmations that make you uncomfortable or that your self talk disagrees with bring you *greatest* value. They are "arguing" with your internal programming, and that programming needs to be changed!

As you read through a script, note the affirmations your self talk argues with and star them. For instance, reading through the *Self Esteem* Script might trigger this "self talk:"

I enjoy being me...................... Sometimes I do.

I treat myself with respect........ Most of the time.

*I trust myself...........................No! I'm always doing things
I don't want to do.

I am proud of being me............Well, yes, for the most part.

In this example, you would star *I trust myself.* After making your tape and listening for at least ten nights, read the starred parts of your script again. If you still argue with those affirmations, compose a clearing script on them. In this example, you would do a clearing script on *trust* — including when you trusted others and were disappointed and when you trusted yourself and were disappointed (see Chapter Three).

Working on one script often leads to other scripts/issues. One tape can serve as a great introduction to another and can lead you into the most valuable script for *you.* For instance, if you don't trust yourself (or others), you are probably not open to receive. You may feel others give to you because they want something from you or because they want to control you in some way. With that belief, you block others from giving to you because you don't want to owe them or be controlled by them. After doing a clearing script on trust, you could follow with affirmations from the *Control* and/ or *Receiving/Being Supported* Scripts.

How to Write Your Personal Script

THE SELF-TALK TECHNIQUE

To develop a completely personal script, decide what you want to change in your mind and your life, and get a working goal statement. Let's say you want to write a best seller. Write that goal statement on a blank piece of paper — *Change Your Mind is a how-to best seller* — and list each self talk thought, image, or feeling you have. Take your time, and let your mind float and wander freely, jotting down your reactions:

I don't know enough; I'm not an expert; I don't have enough time; writing is hard and lonely work.

Your personal script is a combination clearing script (Chapter Three) and rewrite of your negative self talk.

The Clearing Script

Writing and I are one.
Writing Change Your Mind and I are one.
I now release and forgive myself for writing Change Your Mind.
I now release and forgive myself for not writing Change Your Mind.
I now transcend writing Change Your Mind.
Writing a best seller and I are one.
I now release and forgive myself for writing a best seller.
I now release and forgive myself for not writing a best seller.
I now transcend writing a best seller.

Rewriting negative self talk:

Self talk: I don't know enough; I'm not an expert.
Rewrite:

I am guided to the information I need to write Change Your Mind.
I learn all I need to know to write Change Your Mind.
I am the expert in Change Your Mind.
My research has been through observation and is valid.
I present my material simply and clearly.
I choose the best examples.
I use the best questions and give accurate answers.
What I know helps people help themselves.
I empower myself as I empower others.
I empower others to self-heal.

(Affirmations from *Self Esteem* and *Personal Power* could be added here.)

Self talk: I don't have enough time.
Rewrite:

I have sufficient time to complete Change Your Mind.
Writing Change Your Mind is my number one priority, and I act on it.

(Affirmations from *Time Management*, *Action/Completion*, and *Goal Setting* could be added here.)

Self talk: Writing is hard and lonely work.
Rewrite:
> *Writing is fun for me.*
> *I enjoy the time I spend writing.*
> *I feel connected when I write.*
> *I am connected to my work when I write.*
> *I am fulfilled when I write.*
> *I blend writing time with social time easily and effortlessly.*
> *I balance my writing time with my people time perfectly.*
> *Writing has all positive outcomes for me now.*
> *Writing Change Your Mind has all positive outcomes for me now.*
> *Writing a best seller has all positive outcomes for me now.*

(Affirmations from *Writing* and *Success* could be added here.)

THE SO WHAT? AND WHY? TECHNIQUE:

Another technique for writing affirmations is the "so what?" and "why?" technique. Identify what you want, and ask yourself a series of so what and why questions:

Perhaps you have a "want" in your professional life.
I want a better job.

Why?	Because I don't like what I'm doing.
Why?	Because it's boring.
So what?	So I don't feel good when I'm at work.
So what?	So I don't feel like I'm doing anything important.
So what?	So I don't feel like I'm important.

Affirmations could be:
> *I have the most appropriate job now.*
> *My job is appropriate for my style of thinking.*
> *My job is appropriate for my style of living.*
> *My job is appropriate for my abilities, talents, and gifts.*
> *My job is one of my greatest pleasures.*
> *I enjoy my job.*

17

I like going to work every day.
I am enthusiastic about what I do.
I provide value with what I do.
I feel good about what I do.
I am appreciated for what I do, and I feel it.
I appreciate myself.
I see the importance of what I do.
I see the benefits of doing my job well.

This script may be very different from your past programming. It can *change your mind* about your present job or lead you to seek another one, so don't be surprised with the results. (And don't be disappointed if it takes a few months for all of this to materialize in your life.)

Perhaps you have a "want" in your personal life:

I want to have a good relationship

Why?	So I won't be lonely.
So what?	Then I'll feel good.
So what?	Then I'll be happy.
Why?	Because I'll have a purpose for my life.

Write positive affirmations for each of the whys and so whats:
I have love in my life at all times.
I am loving, and I am loved.
I am open to give love.
I am open to receive love.
I give and receive love equally.
I am happy with myself at all times.
I am happy with the people in my life.
I am attracting positive healthy relationships.
I am attracting fulfilling nurturing relationships.
I am at peace with who I am and what I do.
I am happy with who I am and who I am becoming.
I am now willing to accept my life's purpose.
I have a purpose, and I know it.
I am on my path now.

(Affirmations from *Self Esteem, Relationships–Intimacy, and Receiving /Being Supported* could be added here).

GUIDELINES FOR WRITING AFFIRMATIONS:
Be simple: The shorter, the better.

Be positive: Focus on the positive outcomes you desire. Eliminate negative phrases. Replace "I won't get into bad relationships anymore" with affirmations like:
I only enter into relationships that are healthy.
I only enter into relationships that are fulfilling.
My relationships have all positive outcomes for me now.

Be here now: Use the present tense.
Replace future tense --"I am going to be happy", which "futures" your outcomes and puts off being happy, with affirmations like:
*I **am** happy.*
*I **am** at peace.*
*I **am** spontaneous and free.*
*I **am** loving and loved.*
This gives your mind/brain the message to make it happen *now!*

Practice: Like any skill, writing affirmations gets easier the more you do it. During the day, make a game out of converting your negative self talk into short, positive, be here now sentences. You can focus on one area at a time. Listen to your self talk about yourself for a week and convert your self talk to positive affirmations. Then listen to your self talk about work for a week, or about money, or about health, or whatever you want to change. Make notes and use your new positive affirmations on your personal tape.

SOME WORDS OF CAUTION
Use positive words and positive concepts. For instance, if you want to quit smoking, write all the positive outcomes from being a non-smoker. Give your subconscious positive ideas. If your goal is to have healthy lungs, use affirmations like:
I breathe deeply and easily.
I inhale clear clean air.
My lungs are free and clear.
My lungs are completely healed.
I choose health and healthy habits.
I know what is best for my health and I do it.

If your goal is to stop smoking and not start eating in its place, say:

Smoking and eating are separate for me now.

Stress and eating are separate for me now.

Boredom and eating are separate for me now (or whatever triggers your smoking/eating).

I nurture myself in all healthy ways.

I eat what is good for me.

I naturally select the foods that add to my health, and they taste good to me.

One stop smoking subliminal being sold today has the affirmation, *Smoking damages my lungs.* Imagine the possibilities if you continue smoking, while your subconscious is programmed that smoking is damaging your lungs!

Play devil's advocate with yourself when you write affirmations, and look at them from all sides. Be careful, but also enjoy the power of working with your own mind/brain!

Questions and Answers

I'm new at this. What if I write the wrong thing and give my mind/brain the wrong message?

I've used several techniques over the years which I developed to correct my personal mistakes! Here are two which have worked for me:

Listen to your self talk about writing a script, and convert your negative statements into positive affirmations. Then record them as part of your first CYM tape —perhaps with the *Self Esteem* script. Some possible affirmations are:

I make the right tape at the right time for myself.

I write perfect scripts for myself.

I use appropriate words in my scripts.

I deal with appropriate issues in my scripts.

I identify the issues easily and effortlessly.

I move through the issues to the appropriate solutions.

I know what to say and how to say it.

I am clear about my desired outcomes.

I phrase my affirmations perfectly.

I feel good about writing my own scripts.

I am at peace being in control of my own process.

I trust myself completely to take care of myself in perfect ways.

I know what's best for me, and I act on what I know as appropriate.

And/or you can write a "protection" and add it to the beginning of each CYM script:

I am divinely protected as I listen to this tape.

I integrate affirmations that are for my highest good, dissolving all else. My mind/brain increases in health daily, accepting the messages that promote that health, and dissolving all else.

My mind/brain/body/spirit is surrounded by healing love, and only healing messages get through.

I am at peace with the healing messages I receive, and I dissolve all others.

Every message I accept into my mind/brain is for my highest good.

I trust _____ to protect me as I listen to this tape.

(Just as you would rewrite any prepared CYM script, rewrite this protection to blend with your belief system and vocabulary.)

How long does it take for my tape to work? . . . for me to see results in my life?

Most situations in your life today are in process — they were set in motion in the past. Changing your mind today will set new situations in process for your future. Some people experience these changes in one day, while others experience change over weeks and months. For me, the scripts on time management, writing, and personal power worked the fastest. However, getting results from my scripts on financial security and career satisfaction continues to increase as I make more and more changes in my life.

When I feel I'm not making progress on an issue, I inventory the events around that issue. If the events causing me dissatisfaction are results of past actions that occurred before I *changed my mind* — such as credit card debt from old charges, time crunches from old commitments, unequal relationships with old friends — I label them "paying for past mistakes." I separate them from the events more recently initiated which reflect my new way of thinking and being.

Where can I learn more about writing affirmations?

Courses are offered in many areas on writing affirmations and creative visualization. You can check your area for those, or you might want to read the following books:

Creative Visualization by Shakti Gawain

The Only Diet There Is by Sondra Ray

What to Say When You Talk to Yourself by Shad Helmstetter

What if you don't know what you want?

Again, use the system to work for you. Write a script about it.

I easily identify my wants.

I easily identify my needs.

I easily distinguish between my wants and needs.

I easily distinguish between my real wants and the wants of others.

I easily distinguish between what I want and what others want for me.

I easily distinguish between my real wants and my past programming.

I had some interesting learning experiences when I began writing scripts. At one point, I decided I wasn't doing what I wanted to in life because I was doing so many "shoulds" and I wasn't sure I even knew what I wanted. I recorded the affirmation *I know what makes me happy and I do it*. After listening to that tape, I took the Dean to lunch (I was teaching at the time, and he was my boss), and I heard myself telling him I was resigning my teaching position because it didn't make me happy. I was as surprised as he was. I was a single parent with few financial reserves and no immediate career plans. Fortunately, he refused to accept my resignation.

To prevent a repeat of that kind of incident, I began adding **as appropriate** to most affirmations. After re-writing and re-recording that affirmation as *I know what makes me happy and I do it* ***as appropriate***, I devised a two-year plan for leaving that teaching position and making a geographic move and career transition so I could become independent. It worked.

How many topics can I cover in one tape? Can I mix up scripts?

As many as you want. Your conscious mind may be worried

about how much your subconscious can take, but your subconscious is fine! Some people limit each script to a few topics and structure each script in an orderly progression from one topic to another (left brain processors). Others throw in various topics as they come to mind and mix up the scripts (right brain processors). Research indicates you process best in the format that is most comfortable for you (see Chapter Six), so do what is comfortable for you.

I've always been told to be specific with my goals. Does that work with these tapes?

Personally, I am not specific with my scripts. I do not use specific dollar amounts, dates, locations, jobs, etc. My standard money affirmation is *My income now exeeds my expenses.* When I want to bring something into my life, I use *I am now attracting the most appropriate next* _____ *(home, career, relationship, etc.).* I add . . .*for the highest good* . . . to many affirmations as well.

Several of my clients have written scripts with specific goals, however, with surprising results.

Renee wanted a pleasant, inexpensive office space for her personal counseling. She listed her specific "I wants" on her tape: the part of town, amount of rent, size of building, color of carpet, size and shape of office, kinds of people working in the building, etc. Within 30 days, she found an office that matched her description.

Sarah wanted to lose ten pounds in 14 days so she could wear a particular dress to a fancy function. She made a tape with that specific weight and the specific date. A few days later, she lost a crown off a tooth. Her dentist was on vacation, and she wouldn't use anyone else, so she endured ten days in pain without solid food. She lost exactly ten pounds in 14 days.

Mary wanted to earn $50,000 a year as an independent consultant. She had earned that much in a previous job, but she was only earning half that in her own consulting business. She made a tape saying she earned $50,000 by the end of the year. The next week, her consulting business decreased dramatically. After much consideration, she decided the only way to make that much money right away was to work for someone else, which she was not willing to do. She changed her tape.

Evidently, using specific goals can have both advantages and disadvantages. If you decide to use specific goals, consider adding a disclaimer such as:

I get what I ask for as appropriate.
I get more than I ask for as appropriate.
This or something better is brought to me now.
I get what I ask for in all appropriate ways.
I get what I ask for in natural and healthy ways.
I get what I ask for in harmonious and loving ways.

I have a favorite book with sayings that are really meaningful for me. Can I use them in my CYM tapes?

Using books as a foundation for scripts is great! I've done that with several of the prepared scripts (*Winning Friends and Influencing People,* for instance). Using other experts to develop scripts leverages your ability to *change your mind* in any desired area.

Read through a book the same way you read through the prepared scripts in this book — with a pen in your hand. Mark the ideas which appeal to you and convert them to *short, simple, be here now* affirmations. You can convert anything . . .how-to books on sports, crafts, and skill building; self help books on winning in life, parenting, doing your own taxes; business books on managing change, leading, delegating...anything.

There is no limit to how you can use the CYM system to improve yourself and your life. Experiment with it, and make it yours!

3

Writing Your Own Clearing Scripts

A *parable:*

In China, a prestigious university professor devoted his life to learning. He traveled to every library and read every book. Having mastered all written knowledge, he turned to the monasteries to learn what had not been written. He began with a pilgrimage to the oldest and wisest living monk and told him his goal: to learn all the monks knew.

The monk asked if the professor had time for tea before the lesson began. The monk handed the professor a cup and saucer, and began pouring the tea. He continued to pour until the cup was full, and continued to pour until the cup was overflowing into the saucer; still he continued to pour until the tea overflowed into the professor's lap.

The professor leapt up, demanding to know what the monk thought he was doing. Surely he could see that the cup was already full, and yet he continued pouring.

"The cup is like your mind," replied the monk, speaking gently. "It is already too full to add what I know."

The clearing script empties your cup so you can refill it. It empties your mind/brain of negative experiences, issues, messages, programming, and scripting so you can refill it with the things you want to be, do, and have. It is a powerful technique to dissolve messages that obstruct your well-being mentally, emotionally, physically, and spiritually. While writing clearing scripts can take longer than writing affirmation scripts, the results are remarkable. This process has been the basis of success for me and for many of my clients. The clearing script is a sequence of sentences:

_____and I are one.
I now release and forgive _____
I now release and forgive _____ for _____
I now release and forgive myself for _____
I now transcend _____

The clearing script is completely personal and is created out of your unique thoughts, experiences, and feelings. Its effectiveness depends on how well you play detective with those thoughts, experiences, and feelings, so take your time writing it. Think about the script format and what you want to clear.

You can write your script alone, thinking and writing. Or you can think and talk into a tape recorder, making notes as you re-listen to the tape. Or you can talk to a friend who takes notes for you. Combine these techniques or devise others. Find a method that suits your personal style.

How To Clear Your Past

Stage One Clearing is clearing the past. You start with your mother. Begin with Mommy and I are one, and then use the name you called your mother (Mom, Ma, Moms, etc.)

Mommy and I are one.

I now release and forgive Mom.

I now release and forgive Mom for _____

Let your mind wander on this sentence, making notes of any negative images or thoughts that come to mind. If you see Mom leaving you to go to work, note it and clear it with

I now release and forgive Mom for leaving me to go to work.
If you resented your mother leaving you to go to work, add the line

26

*I now release and forgive myself for resenting Mom leaving
me to go to work.*

End the sequence with

I now transcend Mom.

When you've finished with Mom, repeat the process with Daddy:

Daddy and I are one.

I now release and forgive Daddy.

I now release and forgive Daddy for _____.

Include each situation that comes to mind, even if it seems
minor or silly to you. For instance, if you remember your parents
were always telling you to clean your plate as a child, include that.
You may still be reacting to that simple scene today, either by
cleaning your plate because you are "supposed to," or not cleaning
your plate because you are defying authority. In either action/
reaction, you are being controlled by an old scene which you can
clear.

After Mommy and Daddy, clear brothers and sisters, aunts and
uncles, grandmothers and grandfathers, and others who played a
significant role in your youth. If you are adopted, include your
natural mother and natural father. If you don't know their names,
say *my natural mother* or *my birth mother* or language which is
meaningful for you. If you had foster care or an alternative living
environment, include your foster parents or alternative caretakers.

Include school teachers, coaches, counselors, childhood friends,
church figures — anyone you remember with a negative event or
feeling. Review your teen years and include any friends who hurt
you, betrayed you, or who you felt were better than you. Perhaps
you had a best friend named Dana who got better grades or had
more friends than you. Clear Dana with

Dana and I are one.

I now release and forgive Dana.

*I now release and forgive Dana for getting better grades
than I did.*

*I now release and forgive Dana for having more friends than
I did.*

I now transcend Dana.

Review your adult life and clear past relationships, husbands
and wives, children, in-laws, etc. Clear past employers and other
authority figures.

The Stage One Clearing Script can be a long script. For some people, it takes more than one tape to complete this clearing, but it is well worth the time. If your childhood was troubled, the Stage One clearing can be emotional for you. Refer to the *Clearing Childhood* script (Chapter Eight) for guidelines. Take your time and relax with the process, knowing you will benefit tenfold from your efforts.

Regardless of your background, include a sequence on Mommy and I are one (see the research in Chapter Six).

How to Clear Your Present

Stage Two clearing deals with today's people, feelings, and conditions that are in your life because of your past experiences and messages. It empties the cup and re-fills it.

For instance, you might be considering making a move but are besieged by indecision, confusion, and values conflict. Start through the clearing script and see what "comes up" in your mind around moving.

Moving and I are one.

I now release and forgive moving.

I now release and forgive Mom for _____ (she might have wanted to move but didn't because she was afraid of starting over in a strange place) *being afraid to move and start over.*

I now release and forgive Dad for _____ (he might have been in the military and moved you all the time) *for moving me too much.*

I now transcend moving.

Put yourself in the script and clear your move and move history. When you are releasing and forgiving your own actions and feelings, clear them both ways: release and forgive yourself for doing it or feeling it and release and forgive yourself for not doing it or feeling it. Your actions today are often based on reactions to events from your past. What appears to be a positive action, like being very stable and never moving, may be a reaction to being moved too much as a youth and associating fear or loss with moving.

I now release and forgive myself for not moving.

I now release and forgive myself for moving. (Perhaps you are afraid of starting over — so you clear that.)

Starting over and I are one.
I now release and forgive myself for being afraid of
   starting over.
I now release and forgive myself for not being afraid of
   starting over.
I now transcend starting over.

This process will neutralize your issues around moving so you can make the best decision without interference from your past. After writing your clearing script, add an affirmation script for what you want to happen. For a script on moving, you might use affirmations like these:

I now dissolve all family issues around moving as appro-
   priate.
I am at peace with my issues around moving.
I make the best possible decision about moving.
I move at the right time to the right place.
I make the best decisions about what to take and what to
   leave.
Everything I do makes the move easy.
It is easy to bring closure to all the move issues.
I release the move to higher purpose.

I used this process after I left a teaching position with the university. I began to doubt my decision and I felt guilty about it. I created a Stage Two clearing script which alleviated my conflict **overnight**. That script is included in this chapter (see the sample scripts).

Situations occasionally arise which are disturbing and do not appear connected to your past. They are present-time disturbances which can be cleared easily and followed with an affirmation script. For instance, I was involved in a lawsuit and required to give a deposition, and I was irritated and nervous. I had no history of lawsuits in my life or in my family, so the situation appeared to be a present-time disturbance. However, using the clearing script technique, I became aware of my negative programming about lawyers and my anger with the legal system. I created a clearing script/affirmation script that alleviated my nervousness and anger **overnight**. When I gave the deposition, I was calm and clear, and I actually enjoyed the process — telling my side of the story and learning how depositions are taken, transcribed, and used. That script is also included in this chapter (see the sample scripts).

Clearing scripts for common situations and emotions are provided in Chapter Eight. Try the ones that are appropriate for you, and as always, modify the script to fit your personal situation.

Sample Scripts

Clearing present situations that are rooted in past situations and issues: this script has mostly emptying-the-cup script, with some filling-the-cup script

Situation: I had resigned my position as Associate Professor of Business and was experiencing guilt and self doubt — though I was certain I had done the right thing for myself.

Reactions to the situation:
Guilt over leaving UAA
Doubts about leaving teaching

Issues: I found family issues around being a teacher, making and keeping commitments, having a secure job and insurance, and leaving a good job. I also had negative issues connected with the "good ole boy" system.

The emptying-the-cup script:
Teaching and I are one.
I now release and forgive teaching.
I now release and forgive myself for teaching.
I now release and forgive myself for not teaching.
I now transcend teaching.
UAA and I are one.
I forgive and release UAA.
I forgive and release myself for being a teacher at UAA.
I forgive and release myself for not being a teacher at UAA.
I now transcend UAA.
The School of Business and I are one.
I now release and forgive the School of Business.
I now transcend the School of Business.
The Dean and I are one.
I now release and forgive the Dean.

I now release and forgive myself for my relationship with the Dean.
I now transcend the Dean.
The Associate Dean and I are one.
I now release and forgive the Associate Dean.
I now release and forgive myself for my relationship with the Associate Dean.
I now transcend the Associate Dean.
The good ole boy system and I are one.
I now release and forgive the good ole boy system.
I now release and forgive the good ole boy system for being unfair.
I now release and forgive the good ole boy system for protecting the incompetent.
I now release and forgive the good ole boy system for punishing performance.
I now release and forgive the good ole boy system for dominating UAA.
I now release and forgive myself for not being part of the good ole boy system.
I now release and forgive myself for being part of the good ole boy system.
I now transcend the good ole boy system.
Authority and I are one.
I now release and forgive authority.
I now release and forgive authority figures who are not fair.
I now release and forgive authority figures who have hidden agendas.
I now release and forgive authority figures who are incompetent.
I now release and forgive myself for allowing them to have authority over me.
I now release and forgive myself for not allowing them to have authority over me.
I now release and forgive myself for having authority.
I now release and forgive myself for not having authority.
I now transcend authority.
Commitments and I are one.
I now release and forgive myself for keeping commitments.
I now release and forgive Mom for making commitments.

31

I now release and forgive Mom for not keeping commitments.
I now release Dad for making commitments.
I now release Dad for not keeping commitments.
I now release and forgive Dad for keeping his commitments to me.
I now release and forgive Mom for not keeping her commitments to me.
I now release and forgive myself for making full commitments.
I now release and forgive myself for not making full commitments.
I now release and forgive myself for keeping commitments.
I now release and forgive myself for not keeping commitments.
I now transcend commitments.
Staying to get the job done and I are one.
I now release and forgive myself for not staying to get the job done.
I now release and forgive myself for staying to get the job done.
I now transcend staying to get the job done.
Leaving a good job and I are one.
I now release and forgive leaving a good job.
I now release and forgive Dad for not leaving a good job.
I now release and forgive Mom for leaving a good job.
I now release and forgive myself for leaving a good job.
I now release and forgive myself for not leaving a good job.
I now transcend leaving a good job.
Time commitments and I are one.
Commitment to UAA and I are one.
I now forgive and release myself for not making a full time commitment to UAA.
I now transcend making a full time commitment to UAA.
Earning a salary and I are one.
I now release and forgive myself for earning a salary.
I now release and forgive myself for not earning a salary.
I now transcend earning a salary.
Financial security and I are one.
I now release and forgive Dad for stressing financial security.
I now release and forgive Mom for not having financial security.
I now release and forgive myself for having financial security.
I now release and forgive myself for not having financial security.

I now transcend financial security.
Having insurance and I are one.
I now release and forgive Mom for not having insurance.
I now release and forgive myself for having insurance.
I now release and forgive myself for not having insurance.
I now transcend insurance.

The filling-the-cup script:
I provide value with who I am.
I provide value with what I do.
I give and receive value equally.
I provide value as a teacher.
I teach what I know.
I teach with who I am.
I teach with what I do.
I recognize the contributions I have made as a teacher.
I recognize the contributions I have made at UAA.
I make commitments to myself first.
I keep my commitments to myself first.
I am committed to myself.
I commit to myself with ease.
I follow through with my commitments to myself in peace and
   harmony.
I now transcend the roads not taken.
I now transcend taking the easy path.
I now transcend taking the road less traveled.
I am now willing to receive money from any appropriate source.
I recognize money is a form of energy that is returned to me for
   my role as a teacher.
I recognize money is a form of energy that is returned to me for
   my role as an empowerer.
I am independent when I accept money.
I am independent when I am on salary.
I am spontaneous when I am on salary.
I am free when I am on salary.
I am provided for at all times in all ways.

Clearing present situations that are part of day-to-day living: This script includes some emptying-the-cup script, and has more filling-the-cup script.

Situation: I was involved in a lawsuit and had to give a deposition. I was irritated and nervous.

Reactions to the situation: Irritation with the way the legal system had handled me and the lawsuit. Nervousness about the upcoming deposition.

The emptying-the-cup script:

The legal system and I are one.
I now release and forgive the legal system for being male dominated.
I now release and forgive the legal system for not protecting me.
I now release and forgive the legal system for being unfair.
I now release and forgive the legal system for putting power above justice.
I now release and forgive the legal system for putting law above justice.
I now release and forgive the legal system for being cold and ineffective.
I now release and forgive the legal system for protecting criminals.
I now release and forgive the legal system for putting down women.
I now release and forgive the legal system for being arrogant
I now release and forgive the legal system for not having compassion.
I now release and forgive the legal system for not having understanding.
I now release and forgive myself for using the legal system.
I now release and forgive myself for not using the legal system.
I now transcend the legal system.
Lawyers and I are one.
I now release and forgive lawyers for putting themselves first.
I now release and forgive lawyers for playing power games.
I now release and forgive lawyers for being intimidating.
I now release and forgive lawyers for being arrogant.
I now release and forgive lawyers for not having compassion.
I now release and forgive lawyers for being cynical.
I now release and forgive myself for using lawyers.

I now release and forgive myself for not using lawyers.
I now release and forgive myself for being intimidated by lawyers.
I now release and forgive myself for not being intimidated by lawyers.
I now transcend lawyers.
Victimization and I are one.
I now release and forgive victimization.
I now release and forgive myself for being a victim.
I now release and forgive myself for not being a victim.
I now transcend victimization.
Depositions and I are one.
I now release and forgive depositions.
I now release and forgive myself for giving a good deposition.
I now release and forgive myself for not giving a good deposition.
I now transcend depositions.

The filling-the-cup script:

I am at home in the deposition room.
I am calm the entire time.
I am relaxed and at peace throughout the questioning.
I listen to each question carefully.
I can see what the lawyer wants me to say with each question.
I flow with the lawyer's style of questioning.
I am at peace with the lawyer's line of questioning.
I am in harmony with the best outcome for each question.
I take my time to answer each question and talk slowly.
I respond appropriately for my case to each question.
I answer quietly and concisely.
I give just enough information.
I come across perfectly for my case at all times in all ways.
I present myself perfectly for my case at all times in all ways.
My facial expression and body language are relaxed and calm.
My tone of voice is always appropriate for my answer.
I breathe deeply throughout the questioning.
I am in touch with my higher self throughout the deposition.
I am fully conscious throughout the deposition.
I stay grounded and centered throughout the deposition.
I am an honest woman and I appear that way.

It is clear I am telling the complete truth.
I am OK with any outcome.
I know things are working for my highest good now.
I trust the Goddess to take care of the lawsuit.
I trust my higher self to take care of the deposition.
I release the deposition to go to its higher good so that I may
  go to mine.

Questions and Answers

Why should I take all this time to write a clearing script? I'm just interested in . . . (making money/going back to school/losing weight/improving my golf game/having more self esteem, etc.)?

It's hard to walk into the future looking into a rear-view mirror. The clearing script ensures that you are focusing forward, not backwards, and it is a major foundation for the CYM program. Try one clearing script, and judge the results for yourself. I'm sure you'll continue using them!

Why should I say Mommy and I are one? (I didn't even know her/don't like her/get along with her fine/took care of that in therapy/don't have an issue with her.)

Chapter Six (Understanding the Research) explains why this exact line is included in the scripts. My experience with various responses to this line indicates that your resistance to saying it is often in direct proportion to your need for it. If you don't even notice the line, you probably don't have much need for it. If you really argue with saying it, you probably have a lot of unresolved issues around your mother that will benefit from a clearing. If you absolutely refuse to say it, you probably need it the most!

But I like my family and had a nice family. Why should I have to clear them?

Including someone in the clearing script doesn't mean you feel negative about them. It acknowledges that they were significant in your life. If they were a positive influence, putting them through a clearing script will make you even more positive about them. If they were a negative influence, clearing them neutralizes that negative so you can be free of the influence. If there is any question of whom to include, include them. It only takes a few seconds, and it can't hurt.

Where did you get the clearing script?

I worked with CYM for two years before the clearing script came together.

I began experimenting with an expanded script of *Mommy and I are one*, putting other words in place of Mommy. I wondered if being at-one-ment with something would bring it into *atonement*.

The first breakthrough on the expanded script was with Joan and Sue, two col'ege roommates. Joan's mother made a tape for Joan's five college classes using the expanded *Mommy and I are one* script. She said *Calculus and I are one, Western Civ and I are one*, etc. for Joan's five classes. The tape was subliminal because the voice was inaudible; the college students only heard the music. Joan played the tape in her dorm room at night and her roommate, Sue, slept to it as well. At mid-term, Joan got A's and high B's in all five classes, and Sue got A's in Calculus and Western Civ., but got C's and D's in the classes she was taking that weren't covered on Joan's tape. That convinced me to add the _____ *and I are one* sequence to the program.

At the same time, I was realizing most people could not fill their cups until they released their past, and most of the time, that releasing involved forgiving someone. I developed a *Releasing/Forgiving* script and added it to the program.

Separately, I was experimenting with a transcendence script. After hearing a presentation on the historical, philosophical and religious definitions of transcendence, I wondered what would happen in my subconscious if I linked transcendence with issues I wanted to rise above. I did a transcendence script: *I now transcend* _____ and got great results!

The final step was combining these elements and trying it. The results with myself and my clients were remarkable, so I continued to work with different concepts and approaches. The scripts in Chapter Eight are a result of that work.

Why do they work?

I don't know. The clearing scripts concept developed as I observed myself and others using them. I've tried to understand what I've observed, but I got results faster than I got understanding. When I became concerned about my inability to explain why they worked, I wrote a clearing script on my own issues around having the answers. It said

> *Being right and I are one.*
> *Understanding and I are one.*
> *I now release and forgive my family for having to be right.*
> *I now release and forgive the educational system for stressing right vs. wrong.*
> *I now release and forgive graduate school for validating statistical research and discounting experience.*
> *I now release and forgive myself for understanding and being right.*
> *I now release and forgive myself for not understanding and not being right.*
> *I now transcend understanding and being right.*
> *Knowing the answers and I are one.*
> *I now release and forgive myself for knowing the answers.*
> *I now release and forgive myself for not knowing the answers.*
> *I now transcend knowing the answers.*

While I was writing this clearing script, I became aware of my negative feelings about people who don't live the principles they teach — people who talk the talk but don't walk the walk -- "gurus" who aren't true teachers. I had been disappointed by self-styled gurus I had met, and I didn't want to become one of them. So I cleared those issues.

> *Gurus and I are one.*
> *I now release and forgive myself for seeking a guru.*
> *I now release and forgive myself for not seeking a guru.*
> *I now release and forgive others for seeking a guru.*
> *I now release and forgive myself for being a guru.*
> *I now release and forgive myself for not being a guru.*
> *I now transcend gurus.*
> *Walking the talk and I are one.*
> *I now release and forgive people who talk the talk but don't walk the walk.*
> *I now release and forgive myself for walking the talk.*
> *I now release and forgive myself for not walking the talk.*

I now transcend walking the talk.
What others have done, I can do.

This script released me from the right/wrong game that we are taught to play, and made me comfortable acknowledging and exploring the CYM system without knowing all the answers. I became comfortable going public with the program, though I hadn't documented and footnoted my case histories.

When should I do the clearing script?

That depends on your personal style. If you like to plunge right into things, do the clearing script first. If you prefer establishing a comfort zone for yourself first, consider starting with the *Self Esteem* and *Change* Scripts to get a feel for the system and a comfort zone with the process. There is no rigid structure for the CYM program. You decide the most appropriate next step in your process, and do it on your schedule. **But please do the clearing script! It is a major key to your success.**

What's the difference between this tape and the scripts in the book?

First, the clearing script is completely personalized. It will be in your words and about your experiences. Second, it is the foundation for your CYM program. It removes the blocks to your increased well-being. Third, it will evoke more noticeable processing on your part.

What does processing mean?

Processing is a term I use to cover the emotions and reactions you have while your mind/brain/body releases your old thoughts, feelings, and patterns. The processing is complete when you feel neutral about the issues on your tape.

What kind of processing can I expect?

People process differently, and in different time frames. Most people find a pattern in their processing. Dick did three CYM tapes before he recognized his personal process. He reported being tired on day one, and starting day two he "wanted nails for breakfast." About 3:00p.m. on day two, everything smoothed out. His process was consistent: each tape he did after that, he experienced his breakthrough at 3:00p.m. on day two.

Marilyn kept a journal while listening to her first tape – a *Self Esteem/Clearing* tape. Day 1: Made tape. Felt myself rebelling against some of the statements. Day 2: Did not use tape. Day 3: Used tape. Had trouble going to sleep. Day 4: Restless night. Was tired all day and didn't feel good. Day 5: Again a restless night and tired all day. Did not feel good about myself. Played tape and couldn't fall asleep. Day 6: Unorganized day but felt all right about myself. Dinner out with friends whose lifestyle I admire, but I didn't envy them. Day 7: Fell asleep right away. Day 8: Felt confident. Well-balanced day. Listened to tape. Good feeling. Day 9: Feel better. Another well balanced day. Day 10: Good day for accomplishing things, taking charge of life. Did not listen to tape. Day 11: Feel good and now I'm in control. (Marilyn had listened to the tape seven nights out of ten but only slept to it two nights.)

Though you cannot predict your process in advance, I have some general ideas based on my observations of myself and others.

Processing by past experience: It seems logical that your processing is in direct proportion to the experiences that you are clearing, and my observations support that. If you were raised in a wonderful, loving, stable, open environment and had a peaceful life, your processing will probably go unnoticed (and your clearing script will be very short).

To the degree your life experiences vary from that scenario, you will probably: (1) have a longer clearing script; (2) not enjoy making your tape; and (3) have resistance to releasing and/or forgiving some people or incidents in your life; (4) have some form of emotional release during your clearing process.

If you have a history of violence or abuse in your past, you can expect noticeable processing, and the first few days you listen to your clearing script may not be your most pleasant days. But once you have processed, *you are through with that issue.* It's worth a few days of emotional discomfort to empty that cup. (See the *Clearing Childhood* script in Chapter Eight.)

Processing time frames: About half the people process in their sleep and never notice. These people often report awakening tired, as if they had worked all night (which they have, of course). Most people complete their processing in three days, but those with significant issues to release can take a week. A very few go ten days.

Men and women appear to have the same processing time for clearing scripts. Both react in one to three days and complete within ten days, though men often complete within three days. Women I've observed take longer to integrate the changes, but this could be because most of the women I observe are working with emotional issues (depression, abuse, relationships) while most of the men I observe are dealing with topical issues (money, achievement, sports performance). I've only observed a few men dealing with abuse issues, while over half of the women I've observed are dealing with abuse issues. The men who have been abusers seem to process the same ways and in the same time frames as the women who have been abused. (This applies equally to servicemen, policemen and special forces men who have killed others in the line of duty.)

Processing by emotional style: You can expect to complete the entire clearing process within ten days. Your method or style of processing will follow your norm, whatever that is. If you respond to emotional situations with anger, you'll probably get angry. If you respond to emotional situations with tears, you'll probably cry. If you respond to emotional situations by withdrawing, you'll probably withdraw.

Mary, a 30-year-old office manager, had coped with difficult situations in her teen years by running away. She did a combination *Clearing* and *Success: Female* script. On day three listening to her tape, she impulsively walked out of her office, got in her car and drove for more than 200 miles. She called me long-distance to report her actions. Laughing, she said she saw her patterns clearly now, and the whole issue and her need to escape were dissolved by the time she returned home.

People who have denied or repressed their emotions for a long time often experience a release of those emotions. They get angry (if they have repressed their anger) or grief-stricken (if they have repressed their grief) or whatever.

Bob, a Southern gentleman manager, did a combination *Clearing* and *Success: Male* script. On day four listening to his tape, he called a meeting of his staff, climbed on the conference table, and yelled that he knew what the staff had been doing for six months and he wasn't going to let them get away with it any more. They were quite surprised with his outburst, as he was.

41

When he recovered from his embarrassment, he reported he was glad he did it. He re-established his leadership, and his staff took new directions.

Grace had a kidney disease and recorded the *Healing: Christian* script. She became exhausted and sad and cried for three days. I learned her husband had died a year before and she had not accepted his death or grieved it. The healing tape triggered her grieving, which lasted seven days.

Processing by brain type: The left brain processors (logical, sequential thinkers; verbal expressers) often process verbally. They talk about each issue as it clears, and once they have discussed it, the issue is neutralized.

A left-brained couple, Mark and Mary, did their clearing tapes the same week. At dinner on the fifth night, they talked about each issue that was being cleared. Then they looked at each other and said, "Why are we talking about this? Who cares about this old stuff?" They've been neutral about those issues ever since.

The right-brain processors (visual, emotive, creative) often process in images. They see pictures float up from the past, see old scenes, dream about the people and issues involved. Once visualized, they seem to be clear.

The more extreme right-brainers (about 2 to 5% of the people I have observed) seem to process in bad dreams or nightmares. Often, one person or issue clears per nightmare, which could create several nights of bad dreams.

Jane was clearing incest issues, and she dreamed about each involved family member — one per night — seeing herself killing him and then deciding if she wanted to attend his funeral. The nightmares disturbed her waking mind, but she kept listening to her tape until they were all cleared. Jane is confident and self-determined now, and rebuilding her personal and professional life in healthy ways.

Processing by gender: There appears to be a gender-based processing pattern as well. At least 60% of the men I have observed go into denial about the tape working.

John came in because he did nothing but "veg out." He was on worker's compensation, which covered his subsistence living, and supposedly worked as a real estate agent. However, John said he really spent his days going from the TV to the refrigerator and back. He had no direction, no motivation and no joy. We did some scripts for him. On the tenth day, he told me the tape wasn't working. He was very angry about wasting money on a tape that wasn't working because he needed the money for his house payment. I asked him how much TV he was watching each day now, and he exploded, "Watch TV! Why would I watch TV? There's nothing worth watching on TV. I've got too much to do to watch TV." John made one tape every ten days, and by the thirtieth day he was expressing impatience that he didn't have everything in place yet — he had so many plans.

About 10% of the men I've observed deny ever *hearing* the tape, much less having it work. Roy made a tape, and then called me on mornings one, two and three to say he hadn't heard his tape yet. We decided he had so much resistance he was forgetting to put the tape on at night, though the recorder was right beside his bed. On the fourth morning, he reported he had still not heard his tape —at least as far as he was concerned. But he wanted me to know that he found his tape recorder in pieces on the floor across the room from his bed that morning, where it had apparently been smashed against the wall. (He was a former CIA agent who had spent years controlling his emotions—primarily fear and anger.) An interesting side note about Roy: he had worked extensively with hypnosis. His intellectual understanding of the brain and how to program it did not change the intensity of his emotional processing, nor the need for his clearing.

How long should I listen?

Listen at least ten nights. If you want to listen longer, do so. If you want to stop then, stop. Your mind/brain will give you the signals. If you start forgetting to put your tape on, fine. If you are regular in listening to it, fine. Just be sure you have heard it ten nights. (If you skip a night or more, add a few nights longer and listen for 13 or 15 nights.)

A clearing script can create tiredness, irritability, anger, grief and other emotions. This is a sign you are clearing the negative; it is a natural part of the process. Don't stop listening to your tape if you experience these emotions. Know they will be over soon, and the issue you are clearing will be over for good.

43

How will I know when it has worked?

Your clearing tape has worked when you no longer react emotionally to a situation that would have created a negative response from you before. You may continue the mental habit of thinking about that issue but you will not have any feelings about it.

Charlotte wrote me about her first clearing script: "I have not listened to my tape except in my sleep. Today as I sat down to write you and write another script, I picked up my clearing script to go over it. I couldn't do it. As I started to read it, it became boring, and I threw it away."

May all of your negative past become just too boring for you to read or go over again!

Recording Your Own Tape:
Simple Technical Instructions

Assemble the following things to make your tape:

1. A go-to-sleep introduction
2. A *Change Your Mind* script
3. A *Change Your Mind* music tape
4. A blank tape
5. A sound-over-sound recording machine or two cassette recorders

Optional: microphone, earphones

1. A Go-To-Sleep Introduction

You go to sleep listening to your CYM tape, so your go-to-sleep introduction is anything that puts you to sleep when you hear it.

The CYM system provides immediate and long lasting re-patterning of your mind/brain. This is done while you are in the alpha/theta brainwave state (your twilight and sleep states). Playing your CYM tape while you sleep assures the success of the repatterning (see research in Chapter Six).

Record a go-to-sleep relaxation introduction on the beginning of your tape and the CYM script (an affirmations or clearing script) next. Then you will fall asleep to the introduction, and your CYM script will play while you sleep. Your tape is supraliminal because you can hear your voice, and it is also subliminal because you listen to it while you sleep. This differs from most commercial tapes which are solely subliminal because you can't hear the voice/script. With CYM, your voice is audible so you can review it at any time (see Chapter Six on research).

Your go-to-sleep introduction is personal. If you fall asleep easily, it can be a few minutes of restful music. If you don't, use a relaxation introduction. You may already have a relaxation tape or technique that you use. You can buy a commercially prepared relaxation tape (try health food stores, book stores, new age catalogs). You can write and record your own relaxation introduction. Or you can use one of the prepared scripts. Anything that puts you to sleep works.

When preparing your go-to-sleep introduction, use the relaxation technique that fits you. There are two kinds of relaxation techniques. (Scripts for both types of relaxation are provided in Chapter Seven.)

Progressive (body) Relaxation: an actual tensing-relaxing of specific muscle groups that leads to physical relaxation.

Meditation (mind) Relaxation: imagination exercises which lead you somewhere in your mind, often taking you down an escalator or on a walk in nature.

While both of these techniques may work for you, research indicates that many people only respond to one type of relaxation. If your body is usually tense but your mind is clear, try a progressive (body) relaxation technique. Conversely, if your mind is usually anxious, try a meditation (mind) relaxation technique. Research indicates that "low suggestibility" people—those who don't take suggestion easily—respond better to progressive (body) relaxation, while people who are suggestible respond better to meditation (mind) relaxation.

If you haven't used relaxation techniques before, experiment and discover your own style. Purchase relaxation tapes and try them, or work with the prepared relaxation scripts in Chapter Seven. Often, you can tell which relaxation works best for you by reading the script and noticing your response. If it relaxes you, it will work. You can have someone read the script to you, or you can record it and notice your response while you listen to your recording.

Your go-to-sleep introduction can be any length — as short as four minutes and as long as 25 minutes — and you can use any background music you like. Again, the CYM tape is tailored to your style and your needs, so enjoy the process.

When I started using the CYM tapes, my introduction started with "As I listen to the music, I begin to relax. I release the tired-ness, the tension, the frustrations of my day." I added a progressive relaxation which included deep breathing and relaxing my shoulders (which are routinely tight). Then I visualized a rubber band stretched tight as it went loose and limp on a table top, and I ended with suggestions that the script made subtle and positive changes in my life. After hearing a few tapes, my mind/brain became "trained" to the relaxation process and responded easily. As a bonus, I was able to relax at will during the day by simply visualizing a rubber band stretched tight as it went loose and limp.

You might receive the bonus of bio-feedback or anti-stress relaxation from your go-to-sleep introduction also. Many people do. Once your mind/brain has repeatedly heard your go-to-sleep introduction, it locks in as a relaxation trigger, and whenever you hear those words or see those images, you automatically relax. Try it. After you have heard your go-to-sleep introduction three or more nights, try it during the day for relaxation. When you are feeling tired, tense, or irritable, repeat a few lines of your introduction to yourself in your mind or out loud (or visualize a scene from it). You will automatically take a deep breath and relax.

After you have chosen your go-to-sleep introduction and recorded it, you are ready to record your CYM script.

2. A Change Your Mind Script

Pre-written scripts are provided in Chapters Eight and Nine, and instructions for writing your personalized scripts are in Chapters Two and Three.

3. A Change Your Mind Music Tape

The music behind your CYM script is very specific. DO NOT SUBSTITUTE. You can purchase the CYM Music Tape (an order form is in the back of the book) or you can create your own music tape using the music bibliography in Chapter Six.

Create a master music tape and do not record over it.

Using the Change Your Mind Music Tapes:

The *Change Your Mind Music Tapes* are orchestral largo music used for accelerated learning based on the Lozanov research (see Chapter Six). They are available from Supertraining Press through a royalty agreement with Superlearning©. Each tape has different pieces of music with a timer tone every eight seconds which signals you when to begin speaking.

Creating your own music tape:

To make your own tape, refer to the music bibliography in Chapter Six. Select the pieces of your choice and record them onto a 45 minute master tape (honoring copyright laws). Design a timing device to alert you to an eight second cadence, as you will be saying one affirmation every eight seconds. You can record a tone onto the music tape, as I have done with the *ChangeYour Mind Music Tapes*; you can use a metronome; you can create a timer clock.

After working with many people and techniques over the years, I believe having an eight second timer-tone on the music tape itself is the simplest. Create what works best for you.

4. A Blank Tape

For your first CYM tapes, use a 90 minute tape. Later, when you're working on a single issue for a quick result (such as being relaxed in an interview), use a 30 or 45 minute tape and focus on that single issue.

5. A Sound-Over-Sound Recording Machine or Two Tape Recorders

It's easy to combine your voice with music to create a CYM tape. You can use a sound-over-sound machine or two recorders.

Using a sound-over-sound machine:

Sound-over-sound machines are dual cassette recorders that mix your voice with music onto another tape. Sony makes the most reliable and reasonably priced models I have used (around $79).

To identify a sound-over-sound model easily, look at the microphone plug-in spot. If it says MIX MIC, that machine is a sound-over-sound model. *Dubbing and sound-over-sound are not the same.*

Once you have located a sound-over-sound machine, check the instructions with it. General instructions for most machines are:

1. Place the function selector of the cassette recorder in the Dubbing-Normal position.

2. Place the CYM music tape in the playing side.

3. Place the blank tape in the recording side.

4. Plug the earphones into the jack that says headphones (optional)

5. Plug the microphone into the jack on the recorder labelled mixing mike. Turn the microphone on.

6. Simultaneously push the *play* and *record* buttons on the blank tape and the *play* button on the music tape.

7. Both tapes should be turning. You will hear the music in the earphones. Begin speaking into the microphone.

Using Two Cassette Recorders:

1. Put the CYM music tape in one recorder (A) and place it close to the other machine (B).

2. Put the blank tape in B.

3. Plug the microphone into B (optional if B has a built-in mike).

4. Push the *play* button on the A machine and the *play* and *record* buttons on the B machine.

5. Both tapes will be turning. You will hear the music. Begin speaking into the microphone.

You're Ready To Record

Begin by recording your go-to-sleep relaxation in a normal voice with natural rhythm. Use CYM music or any background music which relaxes you. If you have a master tape of your introduction, copy it onto the beginning of your CYM tape.

When you have completed recording your go-to-sleep introduction, record your personal CYM script onto your tape over CYM music.

49

Repeat each sentence three times:

> *Mommy and I are one.*
> *Mommy and I are one.*
> *Mommy and I are one.*

Repeat each sentence to an eight second cadencing.

If you are using the Change Your Mind music tape —

> At the sound of the tone, say sentence A.
> At the sound of the next tone, say sentence A the second time.
> At the sound of the next tone, say sentence A the third time.
> At the sound of the next tone, say sentence B.
> At the sound of the next tone, say sentence B the second time.
> At the sound of the next tone, say sentence B the third time.
> At the sound of the next tone, say sentence C.
> And continue this cadencing for the entire script.

If you are using your own music tape, devise a system that tracks seconds so you begin saying your sentences every eight seconds in the following rhythm:

> Second 1–7 — *Everything I do adds to my health.*
> Second 8–15 — *Everything I do adds to my health.*
> Second 16–23 — *Everything I do adds to my health.*
> Second 24–31 — *I increase in health daily.*
> Second 32–39 — *I increase in health daily.*
> Second 40–47 — *I increase in health daily.*
> Second 48–55 — *I am full of energy and vitality.*
> And continue with this cadencing.

Some sentences are short, lasting two to four seconds, and some are longer, lasting six to eight seconds. The length of the sentence is not important, but beginning the sentence on the eight second beat is. If this feels awkward at first, don't worry. The rhythm becomes automatic very quickly. (I can do it without a timer now!)

Sleep to Your Tape

After you've recorded the script, your work is done. Turn your tape on each night just before you go to bed. Your go-to-sleep relaxation will put you to sleep, and your CYM script will play while you are in the alpha/theta brain-wave state.

Listen to your tape at least ten nights.

Don't put any effort into the changes you want—just flow with the process. Your mind/brain is already working for you, making the necessary changes.

After listening to the tape for at least ten nights, you may continue or stop listening; it's your choice. If you are comfortable listening and the tape makes you feel good, continue listening. If you feel you are through, quit. You will know what to do next— make another tape, put a tape on that you haven't heard in a while, stop listening, or whatever.

You will be changing automatically now, so relax and enjoy it.

Questions and Answers

What if I can't go to sleep while the tape is playing?

If you have trouble going to sleep the first or second night, relax and keep listening. On night three, you'll probably go right to sleep. I don't know the magic of *three* with the brain, but on the third night, 98% of the people who have trouble getting to sleep on night one and two go right to sleep. After you have heard your first tape for ten or more nights, your mind/brain is used to the system and automatically responds to subsequent tapes.

How many times a night should I play my tape?

Once is enough. I haven't seen any differences in effectiveness or immediacy of results based on repetitive listening. Some people listen only once. Some people use auto-reverse machines which replay the tape all night.

One engineer hooked up three machines to each other—so one machine triggered the next. He played three 90 minutes tapes each night, all night long. However, we couldn't identify any added benefits with his system.

Can I play it during the day? in the car?

You can, but playing your tape during the day while you're in the beta brain-wave state doesn't provide any additional benefit. Playing it while you sleep during your alpha/theta brain-wave state—twilight and sleep time—by-passes the conscious defense mechanisms, reaches a different processing part of your brain, and locks in your messages quickly (see the research in Chapter Six).

If you're listening to a *Clearing Script*, you probably won't want to hear it awake. The *Clearing Script* deals with your past issues, and your goal is to change things on the subconscious level easily and effortlessly. There's no reason to process your past while you're awake when you can simply sleep through it.

What if I can't listen to it ten nights in a row?

That's OK. Just listen to it a few extra nights for each night you skip. If you skip one night, add two. If you skip two nights, then add three or so. You will know when to stop listening, so listen until you think it's time to quit. There are no hard rules with this system. It just flows with you.

What if I can't hear my voice clearly, or can't hear it over the music?

It doesn't matter. Your tape is subliminal because you sleep to it. It is supraliminal because you write and record it "consciously." It is subliminal because you "listen" to it while you sleep. Even if your voice is inaudible, you "hear" it subconsciously. Most people want to hear their voices clearly and be able to understand what they are saying, but this isn't necessary for the tapes to work.

What quality tape should I use? What if my tape isn't very good quality?

The CYM system is designed to change the brain through words and messages, so the quality of the recording isn't critical. A good quality recording is much more pleasant to hear, but not necessary. It is possible, however, that a better quality recording — with clear music — may help the brain stay in theta longer (some research indicates this).

Note: If you are using frequencies for brain change, the quality of the recording is critical. Tapes designed to do that are very specific about equipment (a minimum of hertz) and have a left-ear earphone and a right-ear earphone so different frequencies can be sent to different parts of the brain. The CYM system can be integrated with these programs very effectively.

How many sentences/affirmations can I get on one tape ?

To estimate how many affirmations you can get on a tape, figure one affirmation for every 24 seconds of tape. Then determine the length of your go-to-sleep introduction and see if your cassette machine is auto reverse.

For instance, if you have a 6-minute go-to-sleep introduction and a 90-minute tape you are playing on auto reverse, you have 84 minutes—or 5,040 seconds—of recording time. You can record 210 affirmations.

(90 minutes - 6 minutes of go-to-sleep intro = 84 minutes)

(84 minutes X 60 seconds = 5,040 seconds)

(5,040 seconds -:- 24 seconds = 210 affirmations)

If you have a 6-minute go-to-sleep introduction and a 90-minute tape you are playing on a regular cassette recorder, you have 39 minutes—or 2,340 seconds—of recording time on each side of the tape. You can record 97 affirmations on each side of the tape.

(45 minutes - 6 minutes of go-to-sleep intro = 39 minutes)

(39 minutes X 60 seconds = 2,340 seconds)

(2,340 seconds -:- 24 seconds = 97 affirmations)

What if an affirmation lasts longer than eight seconds?

Eight seconds is longer than you think, and most affirmations will fit into that time frame. Speak at your normal pace, and if an affirmation exceeds eight seconds, wait for the next bell and talk again. You will have a 16 second cadencing for that affirmation which will work also.

As you practice and get clearer, you write shorter affirmations. Short statements seem to have more impact than longer ones, possibly because they are clearer and more direct. When I was in mid-life career change writing a "next appropriate job" script, my affirmations were running very long because I didn't know what I wanted. I was writing long affirmations like *I now attract the most appropriate next career that provides me financial security and creative freedom for the highest good.* Then a friend gave me the lines

I get the perfect job in the perfect way.
I do the perfect things for the perfect pay.
That said it all.

How long does it take to make a tape?

Generally, a 90-minute tape takes about two hours to record. Take the length of the tape you are recording (30, 60, 90 or 120 minutes) and add 20 to 30 minutes for setting up and testing equipment.

Your first tape may take longer to record because you are familiarizing yourself with the equipment and system. Hook everything up and do a few "testing, testing . . . " sentences to gauge the volume of your music and your voice. Record a few affirmations to get used to the eight second cadencing system. Then relax and read along easily.

You can record your tape in one sitting with a large block of time, or you can do several shorter sessions. If you're a light sleeper, consider making the tape in one sitting. Turning the recording equipment on and off produces clicks on the finished tape that can awaken a light sleeper.

What if someone else can hear my tape?

If you are listening to prepared scripts like *Self Esteem* or *Action/Completion*, great! Check with the other person to see if s/he minds being "changed," and share a copy of the written script to be sure.

If you are listening to a *Clearing Script* or personalized script, use earphones or a pillow speaker. Earphones work if you can sleep with them. If you can't sleep in earphones, try a pillow speaker — an ear-sized speaker that plugs into the earphone outlet on your machine and fits into your pillow case just under your ear. They are available in many electronic shops and are reasonably priced (about $5.00).

Also, once people see your changes, they may ask to borrow your tapes. One woman made tapes for her entire office and passed them around!

May your tapes work so well for you that your friends want to borrow them!

5

Questions?

More Questions and Answers

How long have subliminals been around?

Subliminals are not new. For centuries, they have been used in physical and emotional healing and education. For instance, practitioners of ancient disciplines used a "whispering technique" to help students memorize lessons. The teacher whispered behind other sounds (strong winds, ocean waves, musical instruments) so students couldn't consciously hear the whispered lesson.

But the use of subliminal techniques is still not widely accepted. Subliminal techniques are alternately considered revolutionary, wishful thinking, powerful, snake oil, or devilry — depending on the source. The U.S. educational system does not incorporate the techniques of subliminal learning, as some European systems do, and most health care professionals deny or ignore the possibilities for subliminals in physical and emotional healing.

Nonetheless, subliminals have become big business. Retail sales of $50 million were reported in 1987 for U.S. produced subliminal audio tapes (Natale), and in 1989, one company earned over $20 million in gross sales (Herman).

What is subliminal advertising?

It is something very different in advertising than in the research laboratory (see Chapter Six on the definition of subliminal). In advertising, it originally meant triggering a pleasant thought or association with an ad so the consumer would buy the product. One study involved Chivas Regal and Marlboro. An ad-photo of Chivas Regal scotch whiskey was manipulated to include a "subliminal" naked woman image. The ad with the image got higher ratings for credibility, attractiveness, sensuality, and the likelihood the viewers might buy the product than the ad without the woman image. A similar study with a male sexual image in a Marlboro ad did not score higher ratings, however.

Subliminal advertising has a more subtle side today. One form it has taken is "cinematic product placement" and "plugging" in motion pictures. Movies advertise products "subliminally" by prominently placing them on the screen or by mentioning specific brand names in the dialog. For this placement and plugging, the movie producers receive large sponsorship fees to help finance making the film (Miller).

I heard about a movie theater that flashed messages on the screen to get people to buy popcorn. Did it work?

James M. Vicary, a motivational researcher and amateur psychologist serving as Vice President of the Subliminal Projection Company, supposedly tried this. On September 12, 1957, Vicary held a press conference to announce a six week ad campaign at a New Jersey movie theater to sell popcorn and cokes. Using special equipment, his company flashed messages on the movie screen for 1/3,000 second saying "Hungry? Eat popcorn." and "Drink Coca-Cola." Vicary announced sales rose dramatically, but he never produced sales figures to prove his claims. Evidently, the entire thing was a sales gimmick to promote the Subliminal Projection Company. Vicary coined the term "subliminal advertising" to describe this form of advertising.

I thought subliminals in advertising were illegal? Aren't they?

Yes, and no. The FTC forbids the use of subliminal messages on the airwaves, but no other legal restrictions are in place. Congress has considered legislation for subliminals in other areas but hasn't reached agreement. Some subliminal researchers and audio-tape producers are campaigning for legislation to set industry standards, but many prefer the lack of restriction they now enjoy.

I've heard some stores use subliminals to stop shoplifting. Is that true?

Yes. Subliminals are being used in various business settings. One New Orleans supermarket buried honesty and productivity messages under background music and reversed cashier shortages and stealing, while two others reduced employee turnover (Schroeder). The McDonagh Medical Center used relaxation messages subliminally in the clinic which reduced patient anxiety 60% and eliminated patient fainting during treatment. Two surprising side effects were the development of more harmonious working relationships and the reduction of smoking among the medical staff members. (Schroeder).

I've heard about subliminal tapes that use speeded up voices. Do they work?

Some tapes use accelerated speech, claiming constant repetition at high rates of speed locks in messages. There is no research proving this, however. Normal speech is about 150 words a minute, and studies show that understanding declines rapidly above 300 words a minute. Accelerated speech tapes present subliminal (or subaudible) messages at 2,300 words a minute or more which appears to be ineffective.

I can't believe *Mommy and I are one* works. Give me an example.

See the research in Chapter Six for more information, but here are the findings of one study:

At Queen's College, Dr. Kenneth Parker, an attorney and psychologist, offered extra credit to students taking his law class who agreed to participate in "a study designed to see if subliminal messages can improve academic performance." Sixty students signed up and agreed to receive subliminal programming three times a week just before class from a tachistoscope, a device which flashes a quick, bright light with a written message imbedded in it (usually 4 msec.). The students looked through the eyepiece of the

57

tachistoscope and consciously saw a flash of light while they subconsciously received a message imbedded in the light. They were divided into three groups:

Group #1 got *Mommy and I are one.*

Group #2 got *The Prof and I are one.*

Group #3 got a neutral message.

At the end of the course, the grading was as follows:

Group #1 got A's

Group #2 got high B's

Group #3 got low B's

And after four weeks, Group #1 and Group #2 remembered more of what they had learned than Group #3.

Mommy and I are one has been researched in many other settings with similar results. A few minor exceptions have been found to its effectiveness:

(1) *Mommy and I are one* doesn't work if the mother wasn't called Mommy. Then, the "mother" word must be substituted.

(2) *Mommy and I are one* doesn't work for schizophrenics who have not differentiated from their mothers (Silverman).

(3) *Mommy and I are one* isn't the most effective affirmation for male dart throwers in competition. In that setting, using the sentence *Beating Dad is OK* produced the highest dart scores. Conversely, the subliminal message *Beating Dad is wrong* produced lower dart scores. (If the sentences were given supraliminally, they didn't work at all.)

Why should I make my own tapes when I can buy one for $9.95?

Noted researcher, Howard Shevrin, feels the idea that the same subliminals will work in the same way for everyone is a "large untested assumption", and he is critical of commercial tape producers who claim to have research but can't produce it. He favors strict regulation of commercial subliminal tapes until they are fully tested for results (Natale).

But some of them may work for you, so try them if you wish. Before listening to a commercial tape, examine the script carefully. If the company won't provide a copy of the script (some say it is their trade secret), don't listen. It's your mind/brain! If you find a script you like, try the tape. If it works, try more from the same company. Once you've experienced results using subliminal tapes, try the CYM system and the clearing scripts. The results will convince you to make more tapes for yourself.

I've used subliminal tapes before and they didn't work. Why not?

Subliminal suggestion works, but getting the right message to your mind/brain in the right way is the key to your personal success. There are many possible reasons the commercial tapes didn't work for you:

1. Most commercial subliminal tapes have ten to twelve messages embedded under the music. If one of those messages doesn't click for you, that tape won't work for you.

2. More than 95% of the commercial subliminal tapes are recorded in the male voice (a few are now co-recorded male/female voices). My observations indicate many women don't accept subliminal messages in a male voice. So if you're female, most commercial tapes may not work for you.

3. Some commercial subliminals are well written, but some are poorly written and are totally ineffective, and some are so inferior they actually worsen the conditions they are meant to correct.

4. Some tapes claim to be subliminal that are really music only. There is no recorded message under the music.

Sometimes you can't find the answers to what works and what doesn't, as a 1989 University of Northern Colorado study shows. A weight loss tape from one of the major tape producers was studied for 16 weeks. Sixty people were divided into three groups:

Group A listened to a tape with music only

Group B listened to a tape with music and a subliminal message on weight loss in both a male and female voice

Group C listened to a tape with the same message as Group B, both supraliminally in a male voice, and subliminally in a male and female voice

At the end of six weeks

Group A, the music only group, lost more weight than Group B

Group B, the music and subliminal message group, had no visible trends of weight loss, and some actually gained weight

Group C, the music and supraliminal and subliminal message group lost the most weight (Herman)

The researcher is still trying to find some explanation for this one!

I don't feel good saying these affirmations. Aren't I just lying to myself?

Affirmations contradict the messages you've been given all your life, the "you're not OK" and "you don't deserve" and "you can't do" and "you can't have" messages. If you've been told you have to work hard, saying *My creative mind creates my wealth* probably sounds like "lying" to you. If you've been taught to believe that you're not very interesting or much fun, saying *I have a winning personality* probably sounds like "lying" to you. If you have anxiety making cold calls, saying *I make new friends and gather new information prospecting* probably sounds like "lying" to you.

CYM allows you to determine *what you want to be true for you,* and to repattern your mind with that truth, easily and effortlessly.

Your past thoughts determined your present. If your past thoughts were negative, your present is negative. Your present thoughts determine your future. If you change your present thoughts to positive, then your future will be positive! CYM gives you a simple method to create the future you want.

Is CYM like hypnosis?

In a general sense, yes. There are a lot of technical distinctions between hypnosis and subliminals, but for practical purposes, you can imagine using a CYM tape is hypnotizing yourself and giving yourself hypnotic suggestions.

How will I know if it's working?

Many people program a behavior change they can verify, such as awakening before the alarm clock goes off, to check their progress.

Consider keeping a journal. Date each script and make notes of your behavior and your feelings for three or four weeks. In three months, review your notes.

Listen to feedback from family and friends. They'll probably notice your changes before you do.

Why can't I tell when it's working?

Some people can tell right away, but most of us go through a denial stage. The five stages of change are denial, anger, bargaining, depression, and acceptance. If you're lucky, you go through all five stages in your sleep. Most people I have observed go into denial on the conscious level and don't think the tapes are working, even though their behavior is changing daily.

When I reviewed my goal setting and time management scripts, I decided I must have made them to experiment with the system, as I certainly never needed them! I had already made the changes and integrated them so completely that I couldn't remember my pre-tape behavior (see Chapter Three Questions and Answers section on processing styles).

Can I learn Spanish, math or history this way?

Some people can sleep learn, and some can't. You may be one of the people who can. If you're not, try the Superlearning© system awake to learn the facts, and the CYM system asleep to program yourself to learn easily and effortlessly.

For instance, if you want to learn Spanish, purchase the Superlearning© Spanish tapes (or other tapes of your choice) and listen to them according to the instructions. Do a personal CYM script to sleep to that says *It is fun to learn Spanish. I learn Spanish easily and effortlessly. I feel comfortable learning Spanish. I enjoy listening to Spanish. I enjoy speaking Spanish. It is simple for me to think in Spanish at will. I can understand when Spanish is spoken to me. I hear the intonations of the language.. I mimic the flow of the language. My accent is flawless. I speak Spanish fluidly, etc.*

I've used this combination effectively with people studying for the CPA exam, the Bar exam, the FAA exam, the Morse code exam, and various classes and subjects.

(For more information, purchase the book, Superlearning©.)

Can I make tapes for other people?

The CYM system was designed for you to make tapes for yourself. You can use it to make tapes for others, but I suggest you ask yourself *why* you want to, and be sure your intentions are very clear and very appropriate first.

I've struggled with this decision myself. While I was developing CYM, my daughter was muddling through her teen years. I knew a tape would help her (and me) get through it faster. I tried persuading her to make tapes, but she refused for over a year.

There were days — and weeks — when I was tempted to make a tape and put it on without her consent, but I wanted her to control her own process. I decided not to make a tape for her and she eventually made one for herself.

In some cases, I have made tapes for others — I've given tapes for gifts and I've helped people make tapes for others:

When Deena's husband was hospitalized for a major heart attack, he had complications. Deena recorded a tape for him and played it at the hospital while he slept. On day two, he began crying, and Deena thought he was getting worse (he had never cried before). He cried intermittently for three days, and then steadily recovered. (Healing tapes often trigger emotional release and crying.)

Kim really wanted to help others. She made tapes for her daughter, her partner, her friends, her co-workers. After a year of making tapes for others, she realized each of those tapes related specifically to her issues. She began to face her own issues and began healing herself as she had healed others—a double win!

If you want to make tapes for others more than you want to make tapes for yourself, try the following affirmations: *I put myself first as appropriate. I am loved and accepted when I take care of myself first. I recognize my issues and own them. I recognize when I project my issues onto others. I dissolve projection in all healthy ways. I have the emotional courage to face my issues openly and honestly.*

Can I make tapes for my kids? How young can they be?

Yes, you can make tapes for your kids. First, spend time thinking about why you are doing it and how you want your child to benefit. Discuss it with the child, and involve him/her in the process if possible. Make the tape with a relaxation introduction and put it on when the child goes to bed, or skip the relaxation introduction and put the tape on after the child has gone to sleep.

For young children, I think simple self esteem and school tapes are appropriate. Include *Mommy and I are one, Daddy and I are one,* and each of the family members and extended family members.

I've seen tapes work for a child as young as 2 1/2 years old. Denise did a tape for her son, 2 1/2, who had never slept through the night because of severe eczema. We wrote a simple script about being loved and cared for, sleeping well, and having smooth, soft, cool skin. By day two, the condition improved and he was sleeping better.

Single issue tapes for older children work also. Dolores recorded the wrestling script for her high school son who was competing in wrestling, and he took the state championship!

What about couples? Can we do a couples script?

Absolutely. And I encourage it. You can co-write a script and co-record it to improve your relationship, plan for your retirement, plan your social activities, or whatever.

Some couples co-record by alternating voices. One person says the first affirmation, and the other person follows with the next affirmation. Some couples speak at the same time, layering one voice over the other. Find what works for you.

Co-writing the script is probably half the work! Agreeing on the messages takes time; the recording is easy. Use the word "co-create." *We co-create a loving environment. We co-create an equal partnership. We co-create equal sharing. We co-create open communication, etc.*

Sharon and Dan were changing careers and relocating. They used the following script, and everything went effortlessly!

We creatively brainstorm each issue as appropriate.
We determine the best approach to our transportation
  issues.
We determine the best approach to our house issue.
We determine the best approach to our relocation issues.
We find ways to dispose of our physical property that
  benefit everyone.
We find it easy to bring closure to our move-related issues.
We are now attracting mutually beneficial outcomes for all
  of our issues.
We recognize the best outcomes when they present
  themselves.
We release all outcomes to the highest good.
We release the move to the highest good.
We have a similar sense of our activities.
We have the same view of our priorities.
We share our vision of the future.
We are at peace with our future vision.

We translate our vision into action effortlessly.
We co-develop a plan of action with ease.
We honor each other's viewpoints in the process.
We creatively brainstorm each issue as appropriate.
We see the process as fun.
We support each other throughout the process.
We recognize and accept each other's personal style and idiosyncrasies.
We are at peace with making plans and revising plans.
We are at peace acting without a plan.
We are safe when we are flexible.
We function independently as appropriate.
We function dependently as appropriate.
We co-create our relationship in all positive ways.
We blend our differences in all peaceful ways.
We honor ourselves and each other.
We stand alone in peace.
We stand together in peace.
We are comfortable asking for what we want and what we need.
We give and receive equally.
We nurture ourselves in all healthy ways.
We nurture each other in all healthy ways.
We lovingly co-create a mentally healthy environment for ourselves.
We lovingly co-create a physically healthy environment for ourselves.
We lovingly co-create an emotionally healthy environment for ourselves.
We lovingly co-create a spiritually healthy environment for ourselves.
We co-develop our interest in new age theories, skills, and knowledge.
We support each other in our continuing evolution and growth.
We support each other in our continuing change and personal development.

What about a family tape? Can we make one for the family?

Yes. For a family tape, consider playing it throughout the

house at night. It's hard to find a relaxation introduction that works for everybody; it's easier to put the tape on after you've gone to sleep. Again, *Self Esteem* is a great starter tape!

I want to quit smoking or lose weight. Which script should I use?

These two issues require personal clearing scripts. About 50% of the time, the first script works. About 50% of the time, it doesn't. If you are a moderate smoker/eater, one script may clear the issue for you. If not, you have to find *why* you do it, and take the *why* out. Determine when you started smoking, or when you became overweight the first time, and analyze what was going on in your life. Then create a clearing script for those issues.

If you started smoking at 14 to be accepted by the peer group, do a clearing script (release and forgive any family members who didn't make you feel accepted, etc.) and refill your cup with (1) *Self Esteem*; (2) affirmations about being accepted; (3) affirmations about being happy whether or not you are accepted; (4) affirmations about having plenty of friends and deserving to have friends; and (5) the following affirmations: *Smoking and being accepted are separate for me now. Smoking and having friends are separate for me now. Smoking and feeling liked are separate for me now. Smoking and being one of the gang are separate for me now. Smoking and being social are separate for me now.*

If you became overweight right after you married, you might want to be less physically attractive so you'll be "safe" from temptation or from sexual advances. Do a clearing script, and refill your cup with (1) *Self Esteem, Integrity, Success,* and *Relationships*; (2) affirmations about trusting yourself; (3) affirmations about being safe when you are physically attractive; and (4) the following affirmations: *I am safe when I am attractive. I am safe when I am sensuous. I am safe when I am sexy. I trust myself when I am attractive, sensuous and sexy. My behavior is appropriate at all times.*

I'm ready to make a tape. Which script should I use first?

Good! If you want to jump right in, start with a *Clearing Script*. If you want to get familiar with the system first (relaxation intro, music, cadencing), start with *Self Esteem* and *Change*. If you want to get organized, start with *Goal Setting, Time Management*, and *Action/Completion*.

Each script is personal to you, and the sequence of scripts is personal to you. CYM is designed to be changed, altered, and modified—combined, adjusted, and mixed. It's your puzzle to play with. Assemble it your way.

Will I become dependent on these tapes?

Because the tapes work so quickly and so well, you might use them a lot, but I haven't observed anyone becoming dependent on them. Remember, the more tapes you make, the healthier you get, which means the less dependent upon external sources you become.

If you are concerned about becoming dependent on the tapes, simply write a clearing script/affirmation script to dissolve the issue. Use a format like this:

Dependence and I are one.

I now release and forgive myself for being dependent.

I now release and forgive myself for not being dependent.

I now transcend being dependent.

Being dependent and using the tapes are separate for me now.

I use the CYM tapes at all appropriate times and in all appropriate ways.

I am fully conscious of how and when I use the tapes.

I use the tapes to increase my health.

I use the tapes to create my personal power and strength.

I use the tapes to _____.

What is the best way to use these tapes?

The best way to use the tapes is the way that works for you. I've provided some guidelines based on my observations of others using the system, but you are the only person who can determine how the system works best for you. My purpose is to empower you to self-heal. I believe this system can do exactly that.

The inner journey is a private journey, and you are your own expert. All you need is some guidance, and my hope is that this system and this book provide some of that guidance. Good luck, and go for it!

6

Why Does it Work?
(Understanding the Research)

Subliminals and Supraliminals

Subliminal perception, or the concept of discrimination by the brain without conscious awareness by the person, is a scientific fact. Your brain takes in messages below your level of conscious awareness, and it responds to those messages. "Subliminal perception is not just a 'watered down' version of normal perception . . . but different in kind" as well (Somekh). Laboratory research projects have repeatedly demonstrated that subliminal messages affect your dreams, memory, verbal behavior, emotional responses, drive-related behavior, conscious perception, and perceptual thresholds.

But laboratory research is difficult to decipher because it is loaded with academic stiffness, technical jargon, personal bias, and controversy. Many researchers are arguing about what subliminal research is, while others are using questionable research models to prove their points (flashing obscene drawings to young women and monitoring their dreams for sexual re-enactments). Reading the research often reveals more about the researcher than your mind/ brain!

Among the subliminal researchers, Silverman, Dixon, and Shevrin provide useful and significant findings. Norman Dixon, noted expert in the field of preconscious processing, finds the controversy over subliminal perception within the psychological community to be based on (1) fear of the existence of an unconscious, (2) the threat to personal liberty that subliminal programming implies, and (3) confusion over the specific words used in the research.

For research purposes, the word subliminal means sub-limen, or below the limen. But the limen is a statistical concept technically defined as below the 50% point of classical psychophysics (Zenhausern), or that stimulus value which gives a response exactly half the time (McConnell).

This research definition has little meaning in non-laboratory settings and does not fit research models for subliminal tapes.

In everyday language, the words subliminal and supraliminal are commonly used for sub-threshold (below the threshold) and supra-threshold (above the threshold). Your threshold is your point of conscious awareness. For instance, if you are listening to an audio tape with a spoken message on it, and you can consciously hear the words and understand them, you are receiving a message above your threshold. This is popularly called a supraliminal message. If you can't hear the words, you are receiving a message below your threshold, popularly called a subliminal message.

Most laboratory subliminal research is based on visual experiments which are conducted using a tachistocope, a device which flashes words or pictures onto a screen at intervals of four msec. or less. Very little research has been done on verbal subliminal messages (subaudible messages) in which a voice is embedded under music, ocean waves, or nature sounds so that it cannot be heard. The existing research on subaudible messages/tapes is inconclusive and contradictory, making it difficult to say with authority what works and what doesn't.

Some research has been done on the effectiveness of subliminal vs. supraliminal messages, however, and on the effectiveness of using the two together. Shevrin presents words both above and below conscious detection levels — supraliminally and subliminally — and analyzes the response of brain-waves recorded at the moment each stimulus is delivered. Both supraliminal and subliminal messages cause brain-wave activity, but this does not mean behavior change will follow. One study showed perception could be altered with subliminal messages, but supraliminal messages were necessary to change physical performance such as learning a new sport. To change a sensory task required a combination of subliminal and supraliminal messages (Zenhausern and Hansen).

In addition, research shows that "emotionally laden messages must be shown longer than neutral messages before a subject will respond to them" (Garner), and each of us has a unique subconscious which gives different affective and motivational meaning to the same messages (Poetzl). While this can be strikingly demonstrated in individuals, it has been difficult to repeat in experimental settings (Westerlundh).

Simply stated, each person responds differently to the same subliminal message, making it difficult to generalize about results from any research model that looks for similarities. Each of us has a different and unique set of experiences, beliefs, feelings, and thoughts in our brains (mental patterns) which interact with new messages, whether they are supraliminal or subliminal, and create responses unique for us.

The CYM system incorporates all these factors to create an effective program that works for you. Your tapes are both subliminal and supraliminal and are personally written in language that is meaningful for you. Your brain absorbs your messages easily.

Your Brain

Your brain is the most complex system known in the universe, and over a half million research papers are written each year about what it does and how it works. Weighing 3 1/2 pounds, it contains a mass of 12 billion tiny octopus-like cells called neurons, and each octopus-neuron has nobs which make electrochemical connections with other octopus-neuron nobs in order to pass messages. Each neuron is capable of forming as many as 50,000 connections (called synapses) with other neurons, creating the capability of more than 100 trillion synapses-connectors in your brain. When a synapses-connection is formed and repeated several times, a mental pattern develops, and that mental pattern is unique to you.

A mental pattern is a memory trace formed in your brain tissue to record something which you have experienced several times. As you see, hear, feel, smell, sense, or taste something over and over, your brain builds a recognition pattern of it. When you experience it again, or something like it, your brain activates the existing memory trace (or patterned thinking) and you go on automatic pilot. You use an enormous amount of patterned thinking daily to do routine tasks (like brushing your teeth) which makes your brain processes extremely efficient (and your day easier). However, being on automatic pilot can work against you when a mental pattern is ingrained but no longer desirable and you want to release the old, develop new perspectives and skills, and move forward with change.

In 1929, Hans Berger invented the electroencephalograph (EEG) which graphically charts brain wave patterns in cycles per second (cps), showing the state of the brain at any given second. There are four brain-wave states — beta, alpha, theta, and delta.

The beta state, from 13-25 cps, is the brain-wave state of logical thought, analysis, and action. You are in beta most of your waking hours — when you are thinking, speaking, and doing, and when you are reading this book.

The alpha state, from 8-12 cps, is the relaxation brain-wave state. You are in alpha when you are feeling soothed and calm — relaxing, daydreaming, meditating, drifting off to sleep. In alpha, you have rapid assimilation of facts with heightened memory and healing. Alpha is the door to the subconscious.

The theta state, from 4-7 cps, is a deep meditation brain-wave state. You are in theta when you are in deep reverie or REM (rapid-eye-movement sleep), the dream state.

The delta state is below 4 cps and indicates a deep dreamless sleep.

Theta REM sleep is a puzzling state, because it appears paradoxical and self-contradictory. While your heart rate and breathing are higher during REM sleep (which means light sleep), your muscles are more relaxed and it is harder to awaken from this state (which means deep sleep). Clearly, this brain-wave state has specific mental processing functions, and "it seems reasonable to assume that sleep is a particularly favorable time for strenghtening and consolidating memories" (Kalat). Emotionally determined memories are more affected by subliminal messages (Dixon), making this brain-wave state the most appropriate for changing emotional memories or emotional mental patterns subliminally.

Poetzl's research found that messages given consciously had results consciously, but messages given subliminally emerged in the theta brain-wave state in dreams (called the Poetzl Phenomenon).

By listening to your *Change Your Mind* tapes as you fall

asleep, you introduce your messages in the alpha and theta brain-wave states, bridging the conscious and subconscious. Working with your brain in the theta state, you dissolve mental patterning from the past and create new patterning. During the process, you experience the Poetzl Phenomenon. While listening to your tapes, you have dreams which are symbolic and emotionally significant, though you may not remember them. When you are dealing with intense emotional issues, you may experience nightmares. This is your brain releasing the old mental patterning from your subconscious, and it happens while you sleep.

When you are working with your brain, you are working with a left brain and a right brain which are connected by a massive bundle of nerves called the corpus collosom. Normally, the two brains work in harmony, but each brain has a preferred set of tasks or functions. By measuring the EEG in each brain during different activities, it is possible to track which brain does what.

In general, the left brain processes words, language, numbers, mathematics, analysis, writing, and other logical and linear functions. It prefers serial processing — anything that proceeds step-by-step in logical order, such as making lists. In contrast, the right brain processes color, music, rhythm, spatial relationships, imagination, and other non-linear functions. It processes in parallel — it sees the whole picture at once, such as recognizing faces. The left brain is considered the active mode and the right brain is considered the receptive mode.

It is currently popular to say you are "left brained" if you process in a step-by-step fashion and follow logical patterns, if you think in words and are comfortable expressing yourself verbally, and if you are organized and structured. Most IQ tests measure left brain skills. You may be called "right brained" if you process in an unstructured way, think in pictures, see the whole more readily than the pieces, tell stories to answer questions, and are less structured in your living patterns.

When these left brain/right brain functions are applied to subliminal research, the differences are almost predictable. Right-brain art and science students are more susceptible to subliminal stimuli when the experiment is loosely structured, while left brainers are more easily influenced if the experiment is highly structured (Dougal).

The effect of subliminal stimuli depends on the person's style as well, and right brainers with a more global and intuitive way of thinking receive greater subliminal effects than left brainers who use a more analytical and organized way of thinking (Dougal). Interestingly, subliminal verbal stimuli presented in a random (non-logical) sequence appear to be stored in your brain in the same order as presented for both left brain and right brain subjects, and the stimuli subsequently re-emerge in that same order.

With *Change Your Mind,* you design the program yourself, so it automatically matches your brain preferences. Left-brain processers usually organize their scripts in a systematic and orderly way, listen to the tapes regularly, and monitor the results. Right-brain processers approach the program with less structure, mixing scripts and issues and listening to the tapes in an irregular pattern. Both types get the results they want.

Poetzl's research also found that supraliminal messages activate secondary thought processes or logical left brain processes, while subliminal messages activate primary thought processes or non-logical right brain processes. The *Change Your Mind* system includes both messages — supraliminal because you write and record your own tape, and subliminal because you sleep to the tape — so both thought processes are activated. You get whole-brain change.

You have a lower brain and an upper brain, and research about the left brain and right brain refer to the upper left brain and the upper right brain.

The lower brain, the subconscious brain, resembles a less evolved animal brain. The lower brain also has two sections — the reptile brain and the old mammalian brain, and is alternately called the reptilian brain, the old mammalian brain, the instinctive brain, and the emotional brain. It handles the activities your conscious brain may not be aware of such as body temperature, blood pressure, chemical balances, digestion, etc. It is in charge of ritualistic behaviors necessary for self preservation and reproduction, from breathing and mating to some non-verbal behaviors, as well as the emotional components of fear, anger, and love.

The upper brain, the conscious brain, is the most recent evolution in mammal brains. It is well developed in humans, other primates, dolphins, and whales. It is alternately called the new brain, the rational brain, the intellectual brain, and the cerebral cortex. This brain does the most advanced processing and is the rational thinking brain.

All your brains work together, but because they developed separately, their integration is incomplete. MacClean speculates that the conflict between the three brains — between the drives of instinct and survival with emotion, logical thought, and consciousness — is at the base of some psychological problems.

It is possible the *Change Your Mind* system affects your whole brain, changing the rational thought process, the emotional feeling process, and the ritualistic behavior process, helping eliminate the conflict between these brains and bringing harmony to your thoughts and feelings.

Dr. Lloyd Silverman's research uncovered one key to bringing harmony to these brains. Working with the idea that conflicting wishes in the subconscious brain often underlie mental problems, he began using subliminal messages with schizophrenics. He found he could increase or decrease their symptoms dramatically by using different subliminal messages, and he eventually discovered one short five word sentence which had universal effects given subliminally, yet lost its effectiveness given supraliminally. This sentence became the subject of hundreds of subliminal research projects and has proven effective with weight loss programs, stop smoking programs, alcholism treatment programs, academic achievement programs, etc.

The sentence — *Mommy and I are one.*

Dr. Silverman believes *Mommy and I are one* is a symbiotic fantasy or fantasy of merging, and merging with the "good mother of infancy" is a sort of archetypal experience that paradoxically allows us to become self sustaining individuals.

Mommy and I are one seems to fulfill a number of psychological needs, but its strength may lie beyond psychology. Fantasies of oneness have been interpreted psychologically as an unconscious desire to return to the womb — the pre-birth state of safety and comfort — when we were one with the mother. This state of pre-existence (before the pain of birth and the agony of a separate existence) is considered the unconscious source of religious myths about a lost paradise. Conditions such as alcoholism, drug addiction, violence, and suicide are viewed psychoanalytically as stemming from the unresolved desire to return to this "oneness."

Spiritually, mystics maintain that meditation creates oneness

73

with a cosmic consciousness, and the merging or reconnecting with spirit (God) is at the heart of all major religions. Perhaps *Mommy and I are one* sparks this oneness as well.

Another way to spark this oneness is with music.

The Music and Cadencing

Ernest Chladni, an 18th century German physicist who researched the relation between music and matter, scattered sand on steel discs and observed what happened to the sand when various notes were played on a violin. Only certain areas of the disc resonated to the notes, causing the sand to be shifted into the areas that were not being resonated. The patterns created in the sand were mathematically ordered geometric shapes.

Dr. Hans Jenny extended this research. Working with liquids, metal filings, and powders, he found as the notes ascended the musical scale, the sand patterns became organic, mimicking hexagonal cells of honeycombs and spirals of nautilus shells. Working with a tonoscope, a device that transforms sounds into a visual representation on a video screen, Jenny recorded the Hindi sacred "OM" sound, the world's most common mantra or prayer-chant. The sound produces a perfect circle filled with concentric triangles and squares. Using the same method, he found the final chord of Handel's Messiah forms a perfect five point star.

Other researchers found that 17th and 18th century composers encoded certain harmonics into their pieces. Harmonics are the tones that resonate high above the audible sounds of music and appear to be in harmony with matter — the tones that create the patterns on the discs. Evidently, music with these harmonics can be health enhancing. Leading edge brain research suggests the neurons of the brain resonate to these harmonics, and many believe this music can serve as a bridge to greater personal awareness.

Georgi Lozanov, a Bulgarian physician and psychologist, incorporated this music into his system of learning called Suggestopedia or Suggestology in Europe and Superlearning© in the U.S. Lozanov found that people performing supernormal feats of memory had a relaxed state of body during their heightened state of mind. Their brain waves were at alpha and their heartbeat was slowed. He experimented with classical music to induce that relaxed state (which was much easier than having his subjects practice years of mental yoga, meditation, and mind control to get the same results).

Lozanov studied the "Goldberg Variations" of Johann Sebastian Bach for the appropriate musical key. Count Kayserling, beset with insomnia, commissioned Bach to compose restful music for him, and Goldberg played the music each night on the harpsichord. Goldberg tired of playing the same piece each night and began improvising — or doing variations. It worked, and the count began sleeping peacefully. For this success, Kayserling gave Bach a large gift of gold.

Lozanov studied the Goldberg Variations in his laboratory and found the arias which begin and end the pieces induce a meditative state. He studied other baroque composers — Vivaldi, Telemann, Corelli, Handel — and found that the slower sections (largo sections) of their music did the same. Through analysis, Lozanov showed that each of these sections of music has 60 beats to the minute, the heartbeat tempo. That music tempo slowed the heartbeat and relaxed the body, while leaving the mind completely alert.

Lozanov's next step was to study rhythm and learning. Material presented at one second intervals was retained at a rate of 20%. Using five second intervals, the retention rate jumped to 30%. Going to ten seconds intervals, the retention rate rose to 40%. Americans using the Lozanov system found that the eight second cadencing was most effective.

During the same years Lozanov was developing suggestopedia in Bulgaria, Dr. A. A. Tomatis, an ear, nose, and throat specialist in France, was studying the effect of frequencies on the ear and the brain. Tomatis found the ear is more than just an organ for hearing. The ear forms an essential part of an integrated system which affects motor skills, body awareness, balance and coordination as well as communication, language, language integration, and mental energy. He discovered that what we hear has a profound effect on our state of health, both physically and mentally. Low frequency sounds do us harm while high frequencies are beneficial.

Sound is measured in frequencies and decibels. Decibels measure loudness, and frequencies measure tone. High frequencies and low decibels are beneficial, but what we hear most often is low frequency at high decibels — the noise of traffic, construction, planes, humming office machines, computers, fluorescent lights, popular music, etc. Low frequency noises like these de-energize us, and this noise at higher decibels causes hearing loss, nervous disorders, and a diminishment of brain capabilities.

Tomatis developed the Tomatis Method, a "listening therapy" based on his findings. The therapy requires 100 to 200 hours of listening to specific pieces of music with the lower frequencies filtered out and the higher frequencies enhanced. As a developmental tool, this method has been particularly successful with learning disabled/dyslexics and also those with more serious difficulties such as autism. When used for skills enhancement, the method has proven beneficial for singers, musicians, performing artists, and other professionals.

While the music you will be hearing on your *Change Your Mind* tape does not substitute for this comprehensive therapy, it does provide benefits. Superlearning© music increases the alpha brain-wave state by an average of 6% while you are awake which can increase healing and serve as a bridge to the subconscious (Schroeder). In addition, this high frequency music helps reverse the process of "over-listening" to low frequencies which helps harmonize the nervous system, provide a new level of energy, relieve stress, lower blood pressure, and induce hypersomnia (you require less sleep). By listening to this music while you sleep, you get the bonus of inner ear stimulation and brain recharging while you're creating new mental patterns for yourself!

For more information on the Lozanov method, purchase the book *Superlearning* by Lynn Schroeder and Sheila Ostrander.

For more information on the Tomatis method, contact
        The Listening Centre
        99 Crowns Lane, 4th Floor
        Toronto, Ontario M5R 3P4
        Canada (416)922-1170
                or
        Sound Listening and Learning Center
        2701 E. Camelback Rd., Suite 205
        Phoenix, AZ 85016
        USA (602)381-0086

Music Bibliography

Vivaldi, A.
  Largo from "Winter" from The Four Seasons
  Largo from Concerto in D Major for Guitar and Strings
  Largo from Concerto in C Major for Mandolin, Strings, and
    Harpsichord
  Largo from Concerto in D Minor for Viola D'Amore, Strings
    and Harpsichord
  Largo from Concerto in F Major for Viola D'Amore, Two Oboes,
    Bassoon, Two Horns and Figured Bass
  Largo from Flute Concerto No. 4 in G Major

Handel, G.F.
  Largo from Concerto No. 1 in F (brass)
  Largo from Concerto No. 3 in D (brass)
  Largo from Concerto No. 1 in B-flat Major, Opus 3 (woodwinds
    and strings)

Telemann, G.
  Largo from Double Fantasia in G Major for Harpsichord
  Largo from Concerto in G Major for Viola and String

Bach, J.S.
  Largo from Concerto in G Minor for Flute and Strings
  Aria (or Sarabande) to "The Goldberg Variations"
  Largo from Harpsichord Concerto in F Minor
  Largo from Solo Harpsichord Concerto in G Minor
  Largo from Solo Harpsichord Concerto in C Major
  Largo from Solo Harpsichord Concerto in F Major

The Mind

It is much easier to ignore these facts than to explain them.
Carl Jung

Most people assume the mind is the brain, and the dominant view in bioscience today is that the mind is a product of brain chemistry. However, there is convincing evidence that the mind is non-local and outside the brain and the body. Controversial subjects like parapsychology, human energy systems, kirlian photography, bioenergy, ESP, telepathy, and clairvoyance are being re-examined today within studies on health and healing as more scientific validation is being accumulated on the mind-body connection.

The belief in a non-local mind is centuries old and can be found in most ancient cultures, civilizations, and religions. For 50,000 years, Shamans have believed minds can travel at will, as have Hindus who call this "astral travel" or "soul travel." Larry Dossey, M.D., a student of distant knowing and healing, tells of a patient who suffered a heart attack during surgery for gall bladder removal. After regaining consciousness, she was able to (1) recite the up-coming cases written on the blackboard outside the operating room which she had *seen* and (2) name the surgeons awaiting the next case down the hall in the surgeon's lounge which she had *seen* and (3) report that the chief surgeon was wearing mismatched socks that day which she had *seen* during her operation. "Her reports were flawless — and were even more amazing because she was congenitally blind. The woman had never *seen* anything in her life." (Dossey).

Randy Byrd, M.D. cardiologist at San Francisco General Hospital, studied heart patients in a non-local mind experiment. He divided 400 patients into two groups as they were admitted to the hospital for heart disease. Group One received the traditional medical care, while Group Two was involved in a double-blind experiment. Unknown to the patients, the nurses, or the doctors, Group Two's names were distributed to prayer groups of mixed de-nominations throughout the country, and they received the tradi-tional medical care plus the prayers of total strangers. Group Two excelled in many ways — fewer deaths, fewer requirements for mechanical respiratory support, less pulmonary edema, and less need for antiobiotics. These results led Dr. William Nolen, author of *Making of a Surgeon*, to suggest physicians write in their patients' hospital orders "Pray for Patient Three Times Daily."

If the mind is not local and not bounded by the physical body, then minds are not fundamentally separated from one another and can be one mind. The Gaia hypothesis, an idea first proposed in 1979 by atmospheric chemist James Lovelock and microbiologist Lynn Margulis, suggests the Earth is a living organism which adjusts and regulates itself like other organisms. Earth could have a mind of its own which is inter-connected to human minds. This is called universal mind and affects all living organisms and perhaps mechanical objects as well.

I've seen many things happen with *Change Your Mind* that support these theories, from "miracle" healings to mechanical dysfunctions, and I've seen too many to consider them "coincidences." Personally, I've had music tapes become blank halfway through when I was working on a script I was resisting, though the tape had music on it when I tried another script. I've made supraliminal tapes which became inaudible halfway through, though my recording style stayed the same. I've had tapes which recorded to a certain sentence, and then stopped recording. And I've had many clients experience similar incidents.

Linda, a physician who didn't believe in subliminals, couldn't get her machine to work. The machine worked perfectly for me. We stood side by side with the machine playing continuously and passed the microphone between us, talking sequentially. My voice recorded; hers didn't. When she asked my opinion, I told her I thought her disbelief was creating an electrical block. She thought that was preposterous but agreed to approach the machine with a different attitude, and her next sentence recorded perfectly, as did her subsequent tapes.

John agreed to be a guinea pig for my first Executive Program tape. He had never used a tape, but Carol, his therapist wife, used them regularly. The tape had a brief health section on it, and John was a sugar and junk food addict. I was interested in John's reponse, but I was especially interested in Carol's observations of John's eating habits. Carol set John up with a recorder, new batteries, and the tape, and he went to the guest bedroom for the first night. The next morning, they found the tape had only played half-way through. Carol replaced the batteries, thinking they must have been defective, and started the tape where it had stopped — which was exactly where the health affirmations began.

I've experienced dozens of these mechanical incidents, and there is no explanation for them. Concurrently, I have witnessed some remarkable breakthroughs for people using the tapes, and intriguingly, I've seen distant people affected by a tape about them.

Kathy was returning to college and had math anxiety. She came in for a test taking tape, but the more we talked, the more I felt she had a incident in her childhood that was blocking her natural memory, so we wrote a general clearing script. Two weeks

79

later, her mother called to confess an incident from Kathy's childhood. Kathy's math anxiety dissolved and she got an A in her math class.

David participated in the Executive Program and did a releasing and forgiving on his father. On Father's Day a few weeks later, he sent a card as usual. But this time, his mother called to tell him his father had cried and cried when he got the card. David flew home and had an emotional re-uniting with his father.

Angela did a clearing script on her husband, his emotionally demanding and abusive ex-wife, and her steppdaughter who was cited as the reason for the ongoing conflict. Within three days, the ex-wife stopped her daily phone calls and became conciliatory toward Angela. The relationships continued to improve.

But all the stories I can tell are not as important as the stories you will tell about you and your tapes and what happens when you use them.

Miracle:

An extremely outstanding or unusual event, thing, or accomplishment.

Webster's Dictionary

A natural occurrence that happens before we are ready to accept or understand it.

Glenn Olds

Something I have seen often with Change Your Mind, and the very thing I wish for you.

Teri Mahaney

References

Albrecht, Karl. Brain Power. Prentice Hall; 1980

Amato, I. Muscle Melodies and Brain Refrains. Science News: 202; 1989

Bateson, Gregory. Steps to an Ecology of Mind. Ballantine; 1972

Beasley, Victor. Your Electro-Vibratory Body. Christopher Hills, ed. University of the Trees Press; 1975

Bentov, Itzhak. Stalking the Wild Pendulum. Dutton; 1977

Borysenko, Joan. Minding the Body, Mending the Mind. Bantam; 1988

Brown, Barbara. New Mind, New Body. Harper & Row; 1974

Brown, Mark. Left Hand, Right Hand. David and Charles; 1978

Bryant-Tuckett, R. and L.H. Silverman. Effects of Subliminal Stimulation of Symbiotic Fantasies on the Academic Performance of Emotionally Handicapped Students. Journal of Counseling Psychology 31(3), 1984: 295-305

Buzan, Tony. The Evolving Brain. Holt, Reinhart, and Winston; 1978.

Chance, Paul. Music Hath Charms to Soothe a Throbbing Head. Psychology Today 21: 14; 1987

Changeux, Jean-Pierre. Neuronal Man: The Biology of Mind. Oxford University; 1985

Chopra, Deepak, MD, Quantum Healing. Bantam; 1989

Cousins, Norman. Head First: The Biology of Hope. E.P. Dutton; 1989

Davidson, Keay. Subliminal Learning or Wishful Thinking? San Francisco Examiner: A-1; 1990

Dixon, N.F. Subliminal Perception, The Nature of a Controversy. McGraw-Hill, 1971

Dixon, Norman. Preconscious Processing. John Wiley & Sons, 1981

Dixon, Norman. Subliminal Perception and Parapsychology: Points of Contact. Parapsychology Review 10(3) May/June, 1979: 1-6

Dossey, Larry MD. Where in the World is the Mind? Unpublished paper presented to the Third International Empathy Conference, Guadalaraja, Mexico, 1989

Ferguson, Marilyn. The Aquarian Conspiracy. Tarcher; 1987

Ferguson, Marilyn. The Brain Revolution. Bantam Books; 1973

Garfield, Lael M. Sound Medicine: Healing With Music, Voice, and Song. Celestial Arts; 1987

Green, Elmer and Alyce Green. Beyond Biofeedback. Knoll Publishing; 1989

Henley, Sue. Cross-Modal Effects of Subliminal Verbal Stimuli. *Scandinavian Journal of Psychology* 16, 1975: 30-36

Herman, Art. Interview, May 1990. President, Teachnology, Santa Barbara, CA

Hurley, Thomas J., Jr. Inside the Black Box: New Cognitive View of The Unconscious Mind. Noetic Sciences Review Winter, 1987: 22-25

Johnson, Harold and Charles W. Eriksen. Preconscious Perception: A Re-examination of Poetzl Phenomenon. *Journal of Abnormal and Social Psychology* 62(3), 1961: 497-503

Joseph, Lawrence E. Gaia: The Growth of an Idea. Bantam; 1990

Joudry, Patricia. Sound Therapy for the Walkman. Sound Therapy; 1978

Kalat, James W. Biological Psychology. Wadsworth Publishing Company; 1984

Kihlstrom, J.F. The Cognitive Unconscious. *Science* 237, 1987: 1445-1452

Locke, Steven MD and Douglas Colligan. The Healer Within: The New Medicine of Mind and Body. New American Library; 1986

McAuliffe, Kathleen. Get Smart: Controlling Chaos. *Omni* 12 February, 1990: 42-92

McConnell, James V., Richard L. Cutler, and Elton B. McNeil. Subliminal Stimulation. *American Psychologist* 13, 1958: 229-242

Miller, Mark Crispin. Hollywood: the Ad. Atlantic Monthly: 41-54; 1990

Moore, Timothy E. Subliminal Advertising: What You See is What You Get. Journal of Marketing 46 Spring, 1982: 38-47

Moss, Thelma. The Probability of the Impossible. New American Library; 1974

Natale, Jo Anna. Are Your Open to Suggestion? *Psychology Today* September, 1988: 28-30

O'Regan, Brenda. The Hidden Mind: Charting Unconscious Intelligence. *Noetic Sciences Review Winter*, 1987: 21

Ornstein, Robert E. The Psychology of Consciousness. W.H. Freeman & Co.,: 1972

Ostrander, Sheila and Lynn Schroeder. Superlearning. Dell Publishing Company; 1979

Parker, Jonathan. Bibliography of Subliminal Research. Gateways Research Institute, 1990

Parker, K.A. Effects of Subliminal Symbiotic Stimulation on Academic Performance: Further Evidence on the Adaptation-Enhancing Effects of Oneness Fantasies. *Journal of Counseling Psychology* 29(1), 1982: 19-28

Pribram, Karl. Languages of the Brain. Prentice-Hall; 1971

Roney-Dougal, Serena. The Interface Between PSI and Subliminal Perception. *Parapsychology Review* 12(4) July/August, 1981: 12-18

Russell, Peter. The Brain Book. E.P. Dutton; 1979

Sackeim, H.A., I.K. Packer, and R.C. Gur. Hemisphericity, Cognitive Set, and Susceptibility to Subliminal Perception. *Journal of Abnormal Psychology* 86(6), 1977: 624-630

Schroeder, Lynn and Sheila Ostrander. Subliminal Report: What You Don't Know, Can Help You - or Hurt You (010). Superlearning, 1985

Schurtman, R., J.R. Palatier, and E.S. Martin. On the Activation of Symbiotic Gratification Fantasies as an Aid in the Treatment of Alcoholics. *The International Journal of Addictions* 17(7), 1982: 1157-1174

Schwartz, Marvin and Michael A. Rem. Does the Averaged Evoked Response Encode Subliminal Perception? *Psychophysiology* 12(4) July, 1975: 390-394

Shevrin, H. Subliminal Perception and Dreaming. *The Journal of Mind and Behavior* 7, 1986

Shevrin, Howard. Brain Wave Correlates of Subliminal Stimulation, Unconscious Attention, Primary and Secondary-Process Thinking, and Repressiveness. *Psychological Issue*, Monograph 8(2), 1973: 56-87

Shevrin, Howard. Does the Averaged Evoked Response Encode Subliminal Perception? Yes. A Reply to Schwartz and Rem. *Psychophysiology* 12(4) July, 1975: 395-398

Shevrin, Howard, William H. Smith, and Dean E. Fitzler. Average Evoked Response and Verbal correlates of Unconscious Mental Processes. *Psychophysiology* 8(2), 1971: 149-162

Silverman, L. and F. Lachmann. The Therapeutic Properties of Unconscious Oneness Fantasies: Evidence and Treatment Implications. *Contemporary Psychoanalysis* 21(1), 1985: 91-115

Silverman, L.H. A Comprehensive Report of Studies Using the Subliminal Psychodynamic Activation Method. *Psychological Research Bulletin* 20(3), 1980: 1-22

Silverman, L.H. and Doris K. Silverman. A Clinical-Experimental Approach to the Study of Subliminal Stimulation. Journal of Abnormal Social Psychology 69(2): 158-172; 1964

Silverman, L.H., A. Martin, R. Ungaro, and E. Mendelsohn. Effect of Subliminal Stimulation of Symbiotic Fantasies on Behavior Modification Treatment of Obesity. *Journal of Consult. Clinical Psychologists* 46(3), 1978: 432-31

Silverman, Lloyd H. Unconscious Oneness Fantasies: Experimental Findings and Implications for Treatment. *PH.D.,* 1984

Somekh, D.E. and J.M. Wilding. Perception Without Awareness in a Dichoptic Viewing Situation. *British Journal of Psychology* 64(3), 1973: 339-349

Therapeutic Effect of Oneness Fantasy. *Perspective* 7(4). A.R.E. Press December, 1985

Trevisan, Louise Ann. Beyond the Sound: a Technical and Philosophical Approach to Music Therapy. Nowicki/Trevisan; 1987

Watson, Audrey. Movement and Drama in Therapy: the Therapeutic Use of Movement, Drama, and Music. Plays, Inc.; 1973

Weinstein, Sidney. A Review of Brain Hemisphere Research. *Journal of Advertising Research.*22(3) June/July,1982:59-63

Weinstein, Sidney, Curt Weinstein, and Ronald Drozkenko. Brain Wave Analysis. *Psychology & Marketing*1(1) Spring, 1984:1742

Weinstein, Sidney, Valentine Appel, and Curt Weinstein. Brain-Activity Responses to Magazine and Television Advertising. Journal of Advertising Research 20(3) June, 1980: 57-63

Westerlundh, Bert. Subliminal Influence on Imagery: Two Exploratory Experiments. *Psychological Research Bulletin* XXV(6-7). Lund University Sweden, 1985

Wittrock, M.C. et al. The Human Brain. Prentice Hall; 1977

Zenhausern, Robert and Karen Hansen. Differential Effect of Subliminal and Supraliminal Accessory Stimulation on Task Components in Problem-Solving. *Perceptual and Motor Skills* 38, 1974: 375-378

7

Go-To-Sleep
Relaxation Scripts

Progressive Relaxation: Back and Neck

(Read each sentence once in a normal voice with natural rhythm)

As I lie here on the beach, I feel warm sand under my back and I sink into it. The warm sand under me supports every joint, every muscle, every bone. A warm breeze brushes over me and I smell the clean salt air of the ocean. I see the blue sky, the green palms, the white frothy water. I hear the gulls overhead.

I relax completely and totally. My muscles are loose like a rubber band that has been stretched. My muscles have been stretched and now they relax.

I visualize my spinal cord. I see it in my mind. Starting with the very tip of the coccyx, I move up my back vertebra by vertebra. Each vertebra is sitting neatly on top of the other in perfect alignment. Each disc is in place. I travel up my vertebrae, one at a time. Each one is in perfect harmony with the next.

I reach my waist in the middle of my back. The nerves coming from the lumbar vertebrae are whole and healthy. They spread out from the right side and the left side. They're fat and full and have total freedom. They are free of pressure, free of pain. They are healthy. My muscles relax throughout my whole lumbar area. My pelvis is relaxed.

I travel upward to my lower thoracic vertebrae. They lie in perfect alignment, one gently floating over the other. All my nerves are streaming out from the right and the left, feeding my body with electrical impulses. All those nerves are fully rounded and whole. They come out from each vertebra, totally free and unencumbered. They feel good. They are healthy. Each disc is in its proper place and is full and whole and cushiony.

I move up into the upper thoracic area, and each vertebra is in perfect alignment. The nerves running from them are full and have total freedom. Muscles crisscross my back and run up and down my spinal cord. They are relaxed and loose. I move up into my shoulders and my neck. My cervical vertebrae begin to curve and are in perfect alignment, perfectly balancing one on the other. The nucleus pulposa is full and pink and free. Cushions rest between my vertebrae. On my left side, the

89

nerves that come from my cervical vertebrae are full and healthy. They move out in appropriate ways into my body. Muscles surrounding my left shoulder are like rubber bands that have been pulled tight and then relaxed totally.

My muscles are loose around the nerves that come from my cervical spine. They untighten, they unwind. They allow those nerves to have total freedom and to relax. My right shoulder is relaxed. Nerves on that side are floating in perfect alignment to the very base of my skull. My left shoulder is relaxed. Nerves on that side are floating in perfect alignment to the very base of my skull.

My skull rests comfortably on top of my spinal column. It rotates with perfect ease, from side to side. My neck muscles are loose and they allow free movement. They feel so good, and they are completely relaxed and well. The muscles are warm and loose and comfortable. My head is lying totally supported, totally rested. My scalp is loose and the capillaries are open and allowing blood to feed my scalp freely.

I move down my arms and the blood vessels open and dilate freely. They allow blood into my hands and fingers. My fingers are totally open to the blood supply. The temperature around them is warm and comfortable, as if I were lying on the beach with warm sunshine all over my body.

My body is at peace. My neck, my shoulders, and my back are relaxed. My hips are totally relaxed. I am at peace, and I am sleeping peacefully.

My spinal cord, my nerves, my body, and my spirit are whole and healthy and at peace.

(One client developed this script for a chronic stiff neck and got good results from using it. The name is withheld by request.)

90

Progressive Relaxation:
Muscle Relaxer

(Read each sentence once in a normal voice with natural rhythm)

As I listen to the music, I begin to relax. I release the tiredness, the tension, the frustrations of my day.

I begin to breathe deeply as I relax and release... release... release.

I feel myself release the tension from my face...from my neck...from my shoulders...from my entire body.

I tense my toes as tightly as I can. I curl my toes as tightly as I can. I hold that tenseness. I relax my toes. I relax my toes completely. Ahhhhh.

I tense my toes, feet, ankles, and legs. I make those muscles tense while I relax the rest of my body. I hold that tenseness. I relax and enjoy that feeling. Ahhhhh.

I tense my thighs and buttocks. I make those muscles tense while I relax the rest of my body. I hold that tenseness. I relax and enjoy that feeling. Ahhhhh.

I tense the muscles in the lower back and abdomen. I make those muscles tense while I relax the rest of my body. I hold that tenseness. I relax and enjoy that feeling. Ahhhhh. I relax, unwind, let go, and relax more. I let the tension drain out of every muscle. I let go of all my weight. I enjoy feeling free and weightless.

I tense the upper part of my torso. I tense the muscles in the back and chest. I make those muscles tense while I relax the rest of my body. I hold that tenseness. I exhale as I let go of all the tenseness in those muscles. I let the tension drain out of every muscle. I let go. I feel those muscles unwinding, relaxing, and letting go. I feel all the tightness disappear. I am clear.

I tense both arms and clench both fists. I hold the tenseness. I relax my arms, I relax my hands. I enjoy the release from the tension.

I tense the muscles in my face...my jaw, my mouth, my eyes, my forehead. I hold the tenseness. I relax, smoothing out the wrinkles in my forehead, relaxing my scalp, my eyes, my mouth, my tongue, my throat. I remove all tension and tightness. I feel the difference.

I have let go completely. I relax completely. I unwind completely. I feel the pleasure of peace and calm spread over my body. I feel the warmth spread throughout my body. I scan my body in its relaxed state, and I know it is free and clear. Waves of relaxation wash back and forth from my head to my toes. I am relaxed. I am completely relaxed. With this relaxation, I can easily connect with areas of my subconscious mind.

I am now open to my own suggestions. I listen to my affirmations on a deep level, and they begin to make subtle changes in my daily living. . . I am at peace with my changes. I am ready to accept my true place with universal peace, health, and abundance.

Meditative Relaxation:
The Castle

(Read each sentence once in a normal voice with natural rhythm)

As I listen to the music, my body begins to relax . . . relax . . . relax. I feel as if I'm drifting . . . floating . . . I am completely at peace . . . I am completely safe. As I drift upward, I feel the worries of the day fall away. I am in complete control.

I begin to breathe deeply and an easy relaxing rhythm begins. I am free to explore the beauty, the peace, the joy of my own soul, my own inner castle. Each room in this castle is safe. I choose when to enter each room as appropriate. It is my castle, built by me. I am guided through it and protected at all times by my companion — a being of light who has been with me since the beginning, who knows me, loves me, and guides me to my greatest good.

I am safe . . . safe . . . a clear, impenetrable shield. I am enveloped in light. I am ready. I am secure. I feel strength growing inside me as I start my journey.

I hear my voice. I hear my affirmations. I believe in myself. I know that I am created for good. I will reach my highest good . . . the room at the center of the castle.

I stand in the castle gardens . . . the outer circle. There is a marble bench which overlooks the gardens. The sun is warm. There is a cool breeze. I sit on the bench and look at my castle. I feel so relaxed, so peaceful. My body begins to heal. I am listening to my body. It is now in healthy control, free to reach its highest good.

It is here I begin to shed those things that bind me. I am guided to the perfect knowledge of what I must do.

(This script was developed by Nancy Sullivan after reading St. Theresa of Avila's work on the stages of soul development, *Interior Castle*.)

Meditation Relaxation:
The Escalator

(Read each sentence once in a normal voice with natural rhythm)

As I listen to the music, I begin to relax. I release the tired-ness, the tension, the frustrations of my day. I begin to breathe deeply as I relax and release... release... release.

I feel myself release the tension from my face...from my neck...from my shoulders...from my entire body.

I listen to the affirmations on my tape, and they begin to make subtle changes in my daily life. I am at peace with my changes.

I am on the fifth floor of a building. I am in a lobby area, and the walls all around me are painted a warm orange. I am standing at the top of an escalator. The escalator is silver colored, and it is working smoothly and noiselessly. It is completely secure and dependable. I see my feet in front of the escalator steps as they rhythmically roll down. Feeling completely safe, I take hold of the railing and step on the descending steps. I begin to glide down without any sound.... slowly, safely. I am on a relaxing journey to the inner level. I feel myself unwinding and relaxing....unwinding and relaxing....as I watch the warm orange walls glide past me. I see the large number 5 on the orange walls of the fifth floor. I take a deep breath and exhale slowly. I mentally repeat 5 several times. It is the end of the ride, and I step off.

I see the 4 on the wall of the next floor, and I walk to the escalator and step on. The walls of the fourth floor are painted a yellow-gold. I see the large number 4 standing out against the yellow-gold wall. I mentally repeat the number 4 several times as I glide effortlessly down the escalator. It is the end of this level, and I step off.

I see the 3 on the wall of the next floor, and I walk over to the escalator and get on. The walls gliding past me are a beautiful green, and I enjoy this beautiful joyous color as I glide silently down. I mentally repeat the number 3 several times as I continue to descend. I reach a more pleasant and relaxing area, and I step off.

I see the 2 on the wall of the next floor. The walls of this floor are a beautiful blue, and I feel saturated with the peace of this color. I pause several seconds in this peace before continuing. I feel a sense of harmony and deep inner peace. I mentally repeat the number 2 several times. I walk to the escalator and I step on to descend. Lower . . . lower . . . lower . . . I continue to glide down.

I see the 1 on the wall of the first floor. The walls are a deep purple, and I float in the protection of this color. I mentally repeat the number 1 several times, knowing each time that I am completely safe and protected at this level. I enjoy the color that surrounds me. I step off the escalator into this restful place. I feel very very peaceful, relaxed, rested, and healthy.

I am now at my main inner level. At this level, I can easily connect with areas of my subconscious mind. I am completely relaxed.

I am open to my suggestions. I listen to my affirmations on a deep level, and they begin to make subtle changes in my daily living. I am at peace with my changes. I am ready to accept my true place with universal peace, health, and abundance.

Meditation Relaxation:
The Rainbow Chakras

(Read each sentence once in a normal voice with natural rhythm)

As I listen to the music, I begin to relax. I release the tiredness, the tension, the frustrations of my day. I begin to breathe deeply as I relax and release... release... release.

I feel myself release the tension from my face...from my neck....from my shoulders....from my entire body.

I am walking up a rainbow colored stairway with seven stairs.

I step onto the first step which is pink. I feel the pink step solid under my feet. I see the clear pink color. I feel the pink color. I begin to vibrate with the pink. I am pink now. I am one with my first chakra. I resonate to earthly love and vitality. I am earthly vitality.

I step onto the second step which is orange. I feel the orange step solid under my feet. I see the clear orange color. I feel the orange color. I begin to vibrate with the orange. I am orange now. I am one with my second chakra. I resonate with earthly vitality and courage. I am earthly courage.

I step onto the third step which is golden yellow. I feel the golden yellow step solid under my feet. I see the clear golden yellow color. I feel the golden yellow color. I am golden yellow now. I am one with my solar plexus. I resonate with earthly wisdom. I am earthly wisdom.

I step onto the fourth step which is green. I feel the green step solid under my feet. I see the clear green color. I feel the green color. I am green now. I am one with my heart. I resonate with earthly healing. I resonate with maternal love. I am earthly healing.

I step onto the fifth step which is light blue. I feel the light blue step solid under my feet. I see the clear light blue color. I feel the light blue color. I am light blue now. I am one with my throat. I resonate with mental healing. I am clear articulation and expression.

I step onto the sixth step which is indigo blue. I feel the indigo blue step solid under my feet. I see the indigo blue color. I feel the indigo blue color. I am indigo blue now. I am one with my third eye.   I resonate with emotional healing.   I am emotional calm.

I step onto the seventh step which is violet. I feel the violet color.   I am violet now.   I am one with my crown chakra.   I resonate with spiritual health.   I am spiritual enlightenment.

I am standing on the seventh step now — and I step off the stairs into a corridor which blends all colors into white. I see the white light.   I am surrounded with the white light.   I live in the white light.

I am open to my suggestions. I listen to my affirmations on a deep level, and they begin to make subtle changes in my daily living. I am at peace with my changes. I am ready to accept my true place with universal peace, health, and abundance.

Meditation Relaxation:
Releasing

(Read each sentence once in a normal voice with natural rhythm)

I am lying on a warm beach, with the bright sun overhead. I hear the seagulls, and I smell the salt air. I feel the light breeze, and the warm sun is on my body. I am lying on the sand, and my body is giving in to the sand. I am giving in to the sand. I am safe and secure as I sink into the sand, which supports me completely. I am relaxing. I am releasing. I am surrendering.

I am surrendering my own realness. I am surrendering my own inherent vitality. I am in my body. It is the inside of the One.

I breathe slowly, gently, evenly.

I breathe in the soles of my feet. I appreciate my feet as the part of me that embraces the earth constantly.

I feel the connection between my feet and my head as I breathe, and I bring my breath up from my feet to my head. I appreciate my body and my unity as I breathe.

As my breath reaches the base of my spine, I focus there and follow the vital current up my spinal cord. I am inside my own spinal cord and I flow upward with my breath.

I reach my head, and I focus on my third eye, between my eyebrows.

I exhale out the top of my head.

Beginning again, I breathe in through the soles of my feet and raise the breath through my body, up my spinal cord, and out the top of my head. I exhale.

I feel the circle of life. I surrender to the essence of my body. I feel at home on earth. I feel the billions of cells in my body as I relax.......and release....and surrender.

I am alive, vital, perfect, and relaxed. I relax... I relax... I relax... I release... I release... I release... I surrender... I surrender... I surrender.

(Adapted from Mary Alice Winchell's Releasing exercise: Celebrate Yourself Retreat, Molokaii.)

8

Clearing Scripts

Clearing Childhood

This script is based on Charles Whitfield's book, *Healing the Child Within* (Health Communications, c. 1987). It is for adults who grew up in families with chronic illness, rigidity, lack of support or nurturing, alcoholism, abuse, or any other troubled condition.

Modify the script to fit you and your situation. Use the affirmations that fit your family background. If the words *inner child* don't work for you, try *child within, true self, real self, private self, higher self,* or whatever feels right.

This script can be very powerful if you were raised in a severely troubled family. You might experience deep emotions such as anger, grief, or depression while processing this script. (Some people develop temporary body pains, rashes, and stomach upsets.) These responses are usually intense and short in duration, lasting one to three days. While listening to this script, have a support system in place, get a lot of rest, and drink a lot of healthy liquids. Consider getting a massage or bathing in hot epsom salt baths nightly.

Having a troubled family and I are one.
Having an injured inner child and I are one.
I now transcend my troubled family and injured inner child.
I am safe and protected when I acknowledge my true childhood.
I am loved an accepted when I acknowledge my true childhood.
I am healed and healthy when I acknowledge my true
  childhood.

I release and forgive my family for being inconsistent.
I release and forgive my family for being unpredictable.
I release and forgive my family for being arbitrary.
I release and forgive my family for being chaotic.
I release and forgive my family for being rigid.
I release and forgive my family for being perfectionists.
I release and forgive my family for being compulsive.
I release and forgive my family for being shame-based.
I release and forgive my family for having secrets.
I release and forgive my family for denying feelings.
I release and forgive my family for denying needs.
I release and forgive my family for withdrawing from me.

101

I release and forgive my family for withholding love from me.
I release and forgive my family for putting me in the middle.
I release and forgive my family for not taking me seriously.
I release and forgive my family for breaking promises to me.
I release and forgive my family for raising my hopes falsely.
I release and forgive my family for disapproving of me.
I release and forgive my family for neglecting me.
I release and forgive my family for shaming me.
I release and forgive my family for humiliating me.
I release and forgive my family for degrading me.
I release and forgive my family for criticizing me.
I release and forgive my family for disgracing me.
I release and forgive my family for joking about me.
I release and forgive my family for laughing at me.
I release and forgive my family for tricking me.
I release and forgive my family for manipulating me.
I release and forgive my family for deceiving me.
I release and forgive my family for betraying me.
I release and forgive my family for threatening me.
I release and forgive my family for bullying me.
I release and forgive my family for being cruel to me.
I release and forgive my family for abusing me physically.
I release and forgive my family for abusing me mentally.
I release and forgive my family for abusing me emotionally.
I release and forgive my family for abusing me spiritually.
I release and forgive my family for _____.

(Clear any specific types of abuse such as beating, molestation, incest, etc. Clear the people who did it by name.)
Mommy and I are one.
I now release and forgive Mommy for _____
I now transcend Mommy .
Daddy and I are one.
I now release and forgive Daddy for _____
I now transcend Daddy.
_____ and I are one.
I now release and forgive _____ for_____.
I now transcend _____.
Abuse and I are one.
I now release and forgive _____for abusing me.

I now release and forgive _____for letting me be abused.
I now release and forgive myself for being abused.
I now release and forgive myself for not being abused.
I transcend abuse.
I dissolve all issues around abuse as appropriate.
I dissolve all issues around abuse in healing and natural ways.

Victimization and I are one.
I now release and forgive _____for victimizing me.
I now release and forgive _____for letting me be victimized.
I now release and forgive myself for being a victim.
I now release and forgive myself for not being a victim.
I transcend victimization.
I dissolve all issues around victimization as appropriate.
I dissolve all issues around victimization in healing and natural ways.

Betrayal and I are one.
I now release and forgive _____for betraying me.
I now release and forgive myself for being betrayed.
I now release and forgive myself for not being betrayed.
I transcend betrayal.
I dissolve all issues around betrayal as appropriate.
I dissolve all issues around betrayal in healing and natural ways.

Authority and I are one.
I release and forgive authority figures for being crazy-making.
I release and forgive my family for being crazy-making.
I release and forgive schools for being crazy-making.
I release and forgive the media for being crazy-making.
I release and forgive organized religion for being crazy-making.
I release and forgive _____ for being crazy-making.
I now transcend authority and crazy-making.
I am my own authority as appropriate.
I challenge external authority as appropriate.
I am safe and protected when I challenge authority.

Boundaries and I are one.
I now release and forgive Mom for not teaching me appropriate boundaries.

I now release and forgive Dad for not teaching me appropriate boundaries.
I now release and forgive _____for not having healthy boundaries with me.
I now release and forgive _____for crossing my boundaries.
I now release and forgive myself for not having boundaries.
I now release and forgive myself for having boundaries.
I now transcend boundaries.
I set and maintain appropriate boundaries and it feels good.
I set and maintain healthy boundaries and it feels good.
I am safe and protected when I set and keep my boundaries.
I am loved and accepted when I set and keep my boundaries.

Trust and I are one.
I now release and forgive myself for trusting too much.
I now release and forgive myself for not trusting enough.
I now transcend trust.
I now dissolve all issues around trust as appropriate.
I know when to trust and when to be cautious.
I am guided to choose trustworthy people in all aspects of my life.
I trust myself completely.
I trust my thoughts and perceptions.
I trust my feelings, senses, and reactions.
I trust my own sense of my experiences.
I trust my inner self to guide me.
I trust myself to take good care of myself.
I trust myself to stand up for myself.
I trust myself to protect my inner child.
I trust ____(God, Higher Power, etc.) to protect me at all times in all situations.

My lost childhood and I are one.
I release and forgive my lost childhood.
I acknowledge and honor my lost childhood.
I grieve for my lost childhood in all healthy ways.
I grieve for my lost childhood in all appropriate ways.
I embrace my lost child into my daily life.
I integrate my lost child into my grown adult.
I transcend my lost child and my lost childhood.

It is now safe for me to be a child.
It is now safe for me to grow up.

My inner child and I are one.
I now release and forgive Mom for denying my inner child.
I now release and forgive Dad for denying my inner child.
I now release and forgive _____ for denying my inner child.
I release and forgive myself for denying my inner child.
I release and forgive myself for not denying my inner child.
I now transcend denying my inner child.

Denying my feelings and I are one.
I release and forgive myself for freezing my feelings.
I release and forgive myself for putting my feelings on hold.
I release and forgive myself for becoming numb.
I release and forgive myself for denying my feelings.
I release and forgive myself for not denying my feelings.
I transcend denying my feelings.

I release and forgive my inner child for feeling (choose the ones that are appropriate for you) *scared, mad, sad, lonely, hurt, bored, frustrated, inferior, suspicious, repulsed, shy, confused, rejected, weak, guilty, shameful, empty, isolated, hopeless, helpless, vulnerable, inadequate, embarrassed, etc.* (Put your core feelings through a clearing script: i.e. being ashamed.)
Being ashamed and I are one.
I release and forgive _____ for shaming me.
I release and forgive myself for being ashamed.
I release and forgive myself for not being ashamed.
I now transcend being ashamed.
I express my shame in all healthy ways and I let it go.

I recognize my feelings as appropriate.
I accept all of my feelings as part of myself.
I validate my feelings and myself when I have them.
I acknowledge the importance of my feelings, and I learn from them.
I express my feelings in appropriate ways to appropriate people.
I am in harmony with my feelings.

I identify my feelings, experience them, and let them go.
Experiencing my feelings and being loved are the same for me now.
Experiencing my feelings and being safe are the same for me now.
Experiencing my feelings and being secure are the same for me now.
Experiencing my feelings and being _____are the same for me now.

Having needs and I are one.
I release and forgive others for not meeting my _____ needs
(choose the ones that are appropriate for you) *love, acceptance, support, safety, attention, guidance, respect, validation, belonging, loyalty, trust, freedom, nurturing, etc.* (Put your key needs through a clearing script: i.e. acceptance)
Acceptance and I are one.
I release and forgive _____for not accepting me.
I release and forgive myself for accepting myself.
I release and forgive myself for not accepting myself.
I now transcend acceptance.
I accept myself at all times in all situations.
I maintain relationships with people who accept me for who I am.

I release and forgive myself for identifying my needs.
I release and forgive myself for not identifying my needs.
I release and forgive myself for meeting my own needs.
I release and forgive myself for not meeting my own needs.
I now transcend having, identifying, and meeting my own needs.
I meet my needs in all appropriate ways.
I meet my needs in all healthy and healing ways.
I meet my needs in safe ways with safe and secure people.

I am a nurturing parent to my own inner child.
I nurture myself in all healthy ways.
My inner child is now healed and healthy.
My inner child is now safe and protected.
My inner child is now loved and accepted.

111

My inner child is now supported and nurtured.
My inner child is now joyful and free.
My inner child is now hopeful and trusting.
My inner child is now content and fulfilled.
(Give your inner child the things you wish it had been given as a child.)
My inner child is now _____

My inner child grieves its losses in all appropriate ways.
My inner child is real.
My inner child gets its needs met in all healthy ways.
My inner child is responsible for itself.
My inner child sets clear boundaries.
My inner child knows what is appropriate.
My inner child chooses safe people as friends.
My inner child _____.

I give myself permission to live in balance, giving to myself first.
I give myself permission to live free, and to be me.
I go forward in peace and love, supported and nurtured.

Clearing Conflict

This script is not to remove conflict from your life, as conflict is normal. It is to clear your issues around conflict from past programming so you can deal with it in calm, healthy, productive ways.

For this script, you play detective. Remember how conflict was handled in your home — with denial, dishonesty, passive aggression, etc. Clear those responses and the family members who modeled them to you. Determine how you were treated when you started or were involved in a conflict, and clear that as well. If being involved in conflict makes you feel guilty, consider combining this with the *Clearing Guilt* script.

Conflict and I are one.
I now release and forgive conflict.
I now release and forgive _____ for dealing with conflict with _____.
I now release and forgive myself for dealing with conflict with

    _____.
I now transcend conflict.

I now dissolve all issues around conflict as appropriate.
I now release and forgive _____ for creating conflict.
I now release and forgive myself for creating conflict.
I now release and forgive myself for not creating conflict.
I now release and forgive myself for avoiding conflict.
I now release and forgive myself for not avoiding conflict.
I create conflict in all appropriate ways at all appropriate times.
I am fully conscious when and how I create conflict.
I am fully conscious of when and how people around me create conflict.
I am fully conscious of when and how _____ creates conflict with me.

Having conflict and being angry are separate for me now.
Having conflict and being devious are separate for me now.
Having conflict and being manipulative are separate for me now.
Having conflict and being aggressive are separate for me now.
Having conflict and running away are separate for me now.

115

Having conflict and causing it are separate for me now.
Having conflict and being at fault are separate for me now.
Having conflict and being wrong are separate for me now.
Having conflict and being bad are separate for me now.
Having conflict and being helpless are separate for me now.
Having conflict and losing are separate for me now.
Having conflict and _____ are separate for me now.

I recognize conflict as normal.
I acknowledge conflict as a part of my life, and I accept it.
I embrace conflict as appropriate, and I am at peace with it.
I am loved and accepted when I am involved in conflict.
I am supported and nurtured when I am involved in conflict.
I am calm and confident when I am involved in conflict.
I am _____ when I am involved in conflict.
I trust myself to be _____ during conflict.
I am _____during conflict.

I benefit from conflict in all natural ways.
I benefit from conflict in all healthy ways.
I benefit from conflict in all healing ways.

I have the courage to work through conflict in all natural ways.
I have the courage to work through conflict in all healthy ways.
*I have the courage to work through conflict in all appropriate
   ways.*
I choose when to engage in conflict and when to let it go.
I make my choices for the highest good of all.
*I transform conflict to increased communication as
   appropriate.*
I transform conflict to increased understanding as appropriate.
I transform conflict to increased cooperation as appropriate.
I transform conflict to _____as appropriate.
I transform conflict to win-win.

Clearing Expectations

If one of your common feelings is disappointment with yourself or others, it may be because of your expectations of yourself and others. Modify this script to fit your own situation.

Expectations and I are one.
I now release and forgive expectations.
I now transcend expectations.
I transcend my expectations of myself.
I transcend my expectations of others.
I transcend others' expectations of me.

I release and forgive myself for having expectations.
I release and forgive myself for not having expectations.
I now release and forgive myself for expecting myself to be_____.
I release and forgive myself for not living up to my own expectations.
I release and forgive others for their expectations of me.
I now release and forgive_____for expecting me to be_____.
I release and forgive others for not living up to my expectations.
I release and forgive _____ for not _____ as I expected.

I see my issues around expectations clearly.
I now dissolve all conditioned expectations as appropriate.
I now dissolve all family expectations as appropriate.
I now dissolve all societal expectations as appropriate.
I now dissolve all _____ expectations as appropriate.
I now dissolve all limitations expectations impose.

I am fully conscious of my expectations, and I adjust them as appropriate.
My expectations are all healthy and natural.
My expectations are all positive and healing.
My expectations are all _____.

Others' expectations and how I act are separate for me now.
Others' expectations and how I think are separate for me now.

Others' expectations and how I feel are separate for me now.
Others' expectations and how I do business are separate for me now.
Others' expectations and how I conduct my relationships are separate for me now.
Others' expectations and how I parent are separate for me now.
Others' expectations and _____ are separate for me now.

I recognize my expectations and I honor them.
I am at peace with my expectations.
I verbalize my expectations clearly and simply.
I am at peace with the difference between what I expect and what I get.
I bring my expectations into harmony with my daily living.
My expectations have all positive outcomes for me now.
My expectations take me to my highest good.

Clearing Grief

This script is based on Elizabeth Kubler-Ross' work and is helpful to process any major loss or change due to illness, death, separation, divorce, rejection, desertion, abandonment, abortion, geographic move, career change, retirement, financial reversal, bankruptcy, children leaving home, etc.

(Include any situation you are grieving - past or present.)
_____and I are one.
I now release and forgive _____.
I now release and forgive myself for _____.
I now release and forgive myself for not _____.
I now transcend _____.

Grieving and I are one.
I release and forgive my family for denying grief.
I release and forgive the society for denying grief.
I release and forgive _____ for denying grief.
I now release and forgive myself for grieving.
I now release and forgive myself for not grieving.
I now transcend grief.
I am in touch with my loss and I grieve it.
I understand my need to grieve, and I accept it.
I am in touch with my grief and I welcome it.
I am open to my grief, and I embrace it.
I take the appropriate amount of time to grieve.
I grieve in perfect ways for me.
I grieve with people who are safe and supportive.

Denial and I are one.
I now release and forgive myself for denying _____.
I now release and forgive myself for not denying _____.
I now transcend denial.
It is appropriate for me to acknowledge_____.
I am safe and protected when I acknowledge _____.
I am loved and accepted when I acknowledge _____.
I am _____ when I acknowledge _____.

Anger and I are one.
I now release and forgive myself for being angry.
I now release and forgive myself for not being angry.
I transcend anger.
It is natural for me to feel anger about _____
I express my anger at appropriate times in all appropriate ways.
I process my anger in perfect ways for me.

Bargaining and I are one.
I now release and forgive myself for bargaining.
I now release and forgive myself for not bargaining.
I now transcend bargaining.

Depression and I are one.
I now release and forgive myself for being depressed.
I now release and forgive myself for not being depressed.
I now transcend depression.
I process my depression in perfect ways for me.
I move through my process with peace and serenity.

Acceptance and I are one.
I now release and forgive myself for accepting _____.
I now release and forgive myself for not accepting _____.
I now transcend acceptance.
I accept _____ completely with peace and serenity.
I accept _____ completely with _____.

I am now willing to release _____ to go to its highest
good so that I may go to mine.
I move through my transitions in peace, love, and grace.
I move through my transitions in dignity, love, and under-
standing.
I move through my transitions in clear consciousness.
I give myself over to the spirit of change and transition.
I claim the power of change and transition as my own.
I face my future wise, free, and unafraid.
I face my future _____.

Clearing Guilt

This script is similar to the *Clearing Shame* script and appears to be more meaningful and healing. You might want to combine the two.

Guilt and I are one.
I release and forgive guilt.
I release and forgive my mother for being guilty.
I release and forgive my mother for making me feel guilty.
My mother's guilt and my guilt are separate for me now.
I release and forgive my father for being guilty.
I release and forgive my father for making me feel guilty.
My father's guilt and my guilt are separate for me now.
I release and forgive society for making me feel guilty.
I release and forgive the church for making me feel guilty.
I release and forgive school for making me feel guilty.
I release and forgive _____ for making me feel guilty.

I now release and forgive myself for feeling guilty.
I now release and forgive myself for feeling guilty about

_____.
I now release and forgive myself for not feeling guilty.
I release and forgive myself for not feeling guilty about _____
I transcend guilt.

I recognize guilt for what it is in my life.
I am guided to make appropriate decisions without guilt.
I am guided to do appropriate things without guilt.
I maintain an appropriate life for myself without guilt.

(Add the things that make you feel guilty: standing up for myself, challenging authority, expressing my feelings, telling the truth, expressing my needs, confronting another, being confused, making mistakes, having fun, feeling good, being vulnerable, relaxing, letting go, eating, etc.)
Feeling guilty and _____ are separate for me now.
I now dissolve my feelings of guilt about _____.

127

I accept myself for who I am and what I do.
I support myself completely.
I support my own mental growth without guilt.
I support my own physical growth without guilt.
I support my own emotional growth without guilt.
I support my own spiritual growth without guilt.
I now replace guilt with acceptance and harmony.
I now replace guilt with honest expression and peace.
I now replace guilt with calm and tranquility.
I now replace guilt with _____.

I am at peace with myself and my process.
I am content with myself and my process.
I am joyful with my growth and personal development.

Clearing Negative Feelings

For this script, you play detective. Identify a negative feeling you have often, and think of the times you experience that feeling. For instance, if you feel pessimistic a lot, identify the times you feel it and clear those types of situations. See if you can find a pattern in the times you have the feelings (around money issues, around relationship issues, around trying something new, etc.), and try to remember the first time you had the feeling. Put those situations through a clearing script. Remember who had those feelings in your family and clear them, releasing and forgiving them for modeling those feelings to you. Determine what you say to yourself when you have those feelings, such as "Oh well, there's no use. It won't work," and rewrite that self talk to positive statements.

Feelings: afraid, anxious, angry, ashamed, bewildered, bitter, bored, confused, concerned, defeated, defensive, depressed, detached, disappointed, disgusted, disturbed, edgy, embarrassed, envious, fearful, foolish, frustrated, furious, glum, guilty, helpless, hostile, humiliated, hurt, inadequate, inhibited, intimidated, irritable, jealous, lonely, mean, miserable, neglected, nervous, pessimistic, pressured, puzzled, rejected, resentful, restless, sad, shaky, shy, subdued, tense, terrified, tight, tired, trapped, ugly, uneasy, uptight, vulnerable, weak, worried, etc.

_____and I are one.
I now release and forgive myself for feeling _____.
I now release and forgive myself for not feeling _____.
I now transcend _____.
I release and forgive _____ for being _____ and modeling that to me.
I now release and forgive _____ for _____.
I now dissolve all my issues around being _____.
I am at peace with _____.

Clearing Negative Habits

For this script, you play detective. Identify a habit you want to change, and clear family members or close friends who do it. Think of the first time you started doing it. For instance, if you smoke, think of when you began smoking, and why you did it — to be accepted, to be tough, to feel bonded with someone, etc. Then determine the times you do it now — when you are tired, lonely, bored, afraid, angry, tense, etc. For instance, if you started smoking in school to feel accepted and you smoke now when you are nervous about performing well, script that as

Smoking and being accepted are separate for me now.
Smoking and performing well are separate for me now.
Smoking and being concerned about my performance are separate for me now, etc.

Follow with positive statements about being accepted (consider the *Self Esteem* script) and performing well (consider the *Performing Well* script). Conclude with affirmations about having healthy lungs, breathing clean air, etc.

Note: If the habits are addictions, combine this with the *Clearing-Twelve Step* Script.

I now choose to be fully conscious of my habits.
I am now willing to change my habits as appropriate.
I maintain positive habits and dissolve all else.
I maintain the habits that are for my highest good.
I maintain the habits that nurture and support me in healthy ways.
I maintain the habits that _____
I heal the source of my negative habit and move on.
_____and I are one.
I now release and forgive myself for _____.
I now release and forgive myself for not _____.
I now transcend _____.
I release and forgive _____ for _____and modeling that to me.
I now dissolve all issues around _____.
I now dissolve the urge to repeat old habits and patterns.
_____and _____are separate for me now.

133

Clearing Passive Aggression

Unexpressed anger often becomes passive aggression. Combine this script with the *Assertiveness* script for more complete effectiveness.

If you do not usually feel or express anger, this script can be very impacting and may trigger intense anger while you are listening to it. Begin listening to it on Thursday night so your primary processing will be over the weekend (or during a time you are away from your usual daily routine and/or a lot of contact with other people).

Passive-aggression and I are one.
I release and forgive passive-aggression.
I release and forgive myself for being passive-aggressive.
I release and forgive myself for not being passive-aggressive.
I release and forgive my family for being passive-aggressive.
I release and forgive society for being passive-aggressive.
I release and forgive the church for being passive-aggressive.
I release and forgive _____ for being passive-aggressive.
I release and forgive _____ for modeling passive-
   aggression to me.
I release and forgive myself for being passive-aggressive
   to _____ .
I release and forgive _____ for being passive-aggressive
   to me.
I now transcend passive-aggression.

Hidden agendas and I are one.
I release and forgive hidden agendas.
I release and forgive myself for having hidden agendas.
I release and forgive myself for not having hidden agendas.
I release and forgive _____ for having
   hidden agendas.
I release and forgive _____ for having hidden agendas
   about me.
I now transcend hidden agendas.
I recognize hidden agendas in myself and others.
I dissolve hidden agendas in natural and healthy ways.

Anger and I are one.
I release and forgive anger.
I release and forgive my family for being angry.
I release and forgive my family for expressing anger in
*   unhealthy ways.*
I release and forgive my family for not teaching me about
*   healthy anger.*
I release and forgive the schools for not teaching me about
*   healthy anger.*
I release and forgive the church for not teaching me about
*   healthy anger.*
I release and forgive _____ for not teaching me about
*   healthy anger.*
I release and forgive _____ for teaching me to suppress
*   my anger.*
I release and forgive myself for having anger.
I release and forgive myself for not having anger.
I release and forgive myself for feeling my anger.
I release and forgive myself for not feeling my anger.
I release and forgive myself for expressing my anger.
I release and forgive myself for not expressing my anger.
I release and forgive myself for being angry toward _____.
I release and forgive myself for being angry about _____.
I am fully conscious of my anger and my anger issue.
I recognize anger when it starts and I acknowledge it.
I accept my anger and I express it.
I at peace with having and expressing anger.
I embrace my anger and I honor it.
I express my anger in all healthy ways.
I express my anger at all appropriate times.
I express my anger in all appropriate ways.
I am loved and accepted when I express my anger.
I am supported and nurtured when I express my anger.
I am _____ when I express my anger.
My anger has all positive outcomes for me now.

Clearing Perfectionism

This script can be used in combination with *Clearing Guilt, Self Esteem, Personal Power,* and *Living With Ease* .

Perfectionism and I are one.
I now release and forgive myself for being perfect.
I now release and forgive myself for not being perfect.
I now release and forgive _____ for (wanting me to be perfect, trying to make me perfect, telling me I'm not perfect, criticizing me for not being perfect, etc.)
I release and forgive myself for confusing being perfect with being loved.
I now release and forgive _____ for acting perfect.
I now release and forgive myself for thinking _____ was perfect.
I now dissolve all need to be perfect.
I now dissolve all desire to be perfect.
I now dissolve all issues around perfection as appropriate.
I now transcend perfection.

Covering up and I are one.
I now release and forgive myself for covering up.
I now release and forgive myself for not covering up.
I now release and forgive myself for covering up _____.
I now release and forgive my family for teaching me to cover up.
I now release and forgive my family for covering up _____.
I now transcend covering up.

Pretending and I are one.
I now release and forgive myself for pretending.
I now release and forgive myself for not pretending.
I now release and forgive my family for teaching me to pretend.
I now release and forgive my family for pretending

_____.

I now transcend pretending.

I am objective about my need to be perfect and my strivings for perfection.

139

Being perfect and being loved and accepted are separate for me now.

Being perfect and being supported and nurtured are separate for me now.

Being perfect and being professional are separate for me now.

Being perfect and being respected are separate for me now.

Being perfect and being worthwhile are separate for me now.

Being perfect and _____ are separate for me now.

I recognize my imperfections and I accept them.

I am at peace with my imperfections.

I am at peace with some people disliking me and my actions.

I am at peace with _____ disliking me and my actions.

I am at peace with some people disapproving of me and my actions.

I am at peace with _____ disapproving of me and my actions.

I am at peace with some people misunderstanding me and my actions.

I am at peace with _____ misunderstanding me and my actions.

My self esteem and being perfect are separate for me now.

My self esteem and others' approval are separate for me now.

I am comfortable with my own internal validation.

I recognize the natural perfection in all things, and I accept it.

I recognize the natural perfection in my life, and I accept it.

I recognize the natural perfection in my body, and I accept it.

I recognize the natural perfection in my work, and I accept it.

I recognize the natural perfection in others, and I accept it.

I recognize the natural pefection in _____, and I accept it.

I celebrate myself just as I am.

141

Clearing the Physical Body

This script has been useful for minimizing the effects of physical illness. Add the illness or illnesses that apply to you and/ or your family (arthritis, cancer, M.S., etc.).

This script can be very powerful and often results in anger or grief. While listening to this script, have a support system in place, get a lot of rest, and drink plenty of healthy fluids. Consider getting a massage, and bathe in hot epsom salt baths nightly.

My physical body and I are one.
I release and forgive my physical body for having _____.
I release and forgive my physical body for not having _____.
I embrace _____ and I flow with it.
I am at peace with _____ and with having it in my body.
I transcend having _____.

(If you are clearing a family illness, release and forgive the family for having the illness and passing it on.)
I release and forgive my family for having _____.
I release and forgive my family for not having _____.
I release and forgive my family for passing_____ on to me.
I release and forgive myself for getting _____.
I now give myself permission to break the family patterns that create _____ in our lives.

My body relaxes completely and is free and clear.
My biological body is in balance.
My emotional body is in balance.
My mental body is in balance.
My spiritual body is in balance.
My etheric body is in balance.
My sympathetic system is in balance.
My cerebro-spinal system is in balance.
My glandular secretions are in balance.
Equipoise and I are one.
Ionic balancing and I are one.

My body is a hologram of the infinite.
My body is appropriate for higher purpose.

I am strong and powerful in all my physical manifestations.
I am flexible, limber, and loose in all my physical
manifestations.

My muscles and I are one.
My muscles are healthy and strong.
I now transcend my muscles.
My glands and I are one.
My glands are healthy and strong.
I now transcend my glands.
My body tissues and I are one.
My body tissues are healthy and strong.
I now transcend my body tissues.

My cells and I are one.
I am safe and protected on a cellular level.
I am loved and nurtured on a cellular level.
I am accepted and supported on a cellular level.
I am safe with cellular expansion.
My cellular intake and outgo are balanced at all times.
My cells eliminate waste effortlessly.
I now transcend my cells.
My cellular memories and I are one.
I now transcend my cellular memories.
I am now willing to release cellular memory as appropriate.
My cellular memories yield to consciousness as appropriate for
higher purpose.
My RNA and I are one.
I now transcend my RNA.
My DNA and I are one.
I now transcend my DNA.

My biological body transforms itself as appropriate.
My molecular structures rearrange and transform themselves
as needed for effortless processing.
Emotions flow through my body and out.
Information flows through my body and out.
Processing flows through my body and out.
Accessing flows through my body and out.
Motion flows through my body and out.

Divine love flows through my body and out.
Fluids flow through my body and out.
Solids flow through my body and out.

My body is honest and is in the here and now.
I identify with my body and am one with it.
I am in tune with my body and its messages for me.
I access messages from my physical body in all appropriate ways.
I access messages from my physical body in a timely manner.
I access messages from my physical body fully consciously.
My physical body distinguishes internal messages easily, effortlessly, and in grace.
My physical body distinguishes external messages easily, effortlessly, and in grace.
My physical body neutralizes internal messages as appropriate.
My physical body neutralizes external messages as appropriate.
My body parts yield their messages in peace and love.
Information stored physically now becomes available in all appropriate and timely ways.
My body is available to all realms of information clearly and consciously.
My body is available to all realms of information with ease, peace, and joy.
My body messages dissolve as appropriate, leaving my body clear.
My body is in flow with universal harmony.

My body is in a state of grace at all times.
My body accesses unlimited love in peace and harmony.
My body processes unlimited love with ease and flow.
My body is fully conscious of unlimited love.
My body is unlimited love in action.
My physical body and the higher frequency of the spirit are one.
I now transcend the higher frequency of the spirit.

The divine universe manifests itself through my biological body in all open, free, clear, timely, conscious and loving ways.

Clearing Shame

This script is based on John Bradshaw's theories of shame-based families. It is included because of the current popularity of the theory. Consider combining it with the *Clearing Guilt* script.

Shame and I are one.
I release and forgive shame.
I release and forgive my mother for having shame.
I release and forgive my mother for giving me her shame.
I release and forgive my mother for making me feel ashamed.
My mother's shame and my shame are separate for me now.
I release and forgive my father for having shame.
I release and forgive my father for giving me his shame.
I release and forgive my father for making me feel ashamed.
My father's shame and my shame are separate for me now.
I release and forgive society for being shame-based.
I release and forgive society for making me feel ashamed.
I release and forgive my church for being shame-based.
I release and forgive my church for making me feel ashamed.
My church's shame and my shame are separate for me now.

(Add other people, groups, institutions, etc. here)
I release and forgive _____ for having shame.
I release and forgive _____ for giving me shame.
I release and forgive _____ for making me feel ashamed.
_____shame and my shame are separate for me now.

I release and forgive myself for feeling shame.
I release and forgive myself for not feeling shame.
I release and forgive myself for denying shame.
I now transcend denying shame.
I release and forgive myself for repressing shame.
I now transcend repressing shame.
I release and forgive myself for displacing shame.
I now transcend displacing shame.
I release and forgive myself for acting out shame.
I now transcend acting out shame.
I now transcend shame and shame issues.

I replace denial with acceptance and harmony.
I replace repression with honest expression and peace.
I replace displacement with clarity in calm and tranquillity.

I accept my shame for what it is and I acknowledge it.
I experience my past shame and I embrace it.
Experiencing my past shame has all positive outcomes for me
  now.
I experience my past shame in all appropriate environments.
I experience my past shame in all loving environments.
I experience my past shame in all accepting environments.

I am safe and protected when I experience my past shame.
I am loved and accepted when I experience my past shame.
I am nurtured and supported when I experience my past shame.
I am _____when I experience my past shame.

I experience shame in all appropriate ways.
I experience shame in all healthy ways.
I experience shame in all self accepting ways.
I experience shame in all self loving ways.

Shame and _____are separate for me now.
(Include the things that make you feel ashamed here: procrastinating, dishonesty, divorce, failure, overeating, overspending, abortion, lifestyle, sex, etc.)

I heal and release all my mental memories of shame in peace
  and harmony.
I heal and release all my emotional memories of shame in peace
  and harmony.
I heal and release all my physical memories of shame in peace
  and harmony.
I heal and release all my spiritual memories of shame in peace
  and harmony.

Clearing Struggle

Most of us were taught "life is a struggle." Spend time with this script to uncover your "struggle messages" and clear them. Combine the script with *Living With Ease* for more effectiveness.

Struggle and I are one.
I now release and forgive myself for struggling.
I now release and forgive myself for not struggling.
I now release and forgive _____ for telling me I had to struggle.
I release and forgive society for believing in no pain, no gain.
I now release and forgive _____ for modeling struggle to me.
I now release and forgive _____ for struggling (and making it, not making it)
I now release and forgive _____ for not struggling (and making it, not making it).
I now transcend struggle.

I recognize my issues around struggling and I embrace them.
I now dissolve all my issues around struggling as appropriate.
I now dissolve all my family issues around struggling as appropriate.
I now dissolve all my cultural issues around struggling as appropriate.
I now dissolve all _____ issues around struggling as appropriate.

Struggling and making it are separate for me now.
Struggling and being loved and accepted are separate for me now.
Struggling and being nurtured and supported are separate for me now.
Struggling and surviving are separate for me now.
Struggling and performing well are separate for me now.
Struggling and making money are separate for me now.
Struggling and having a good life are separate for me now.
Struggling and _____ are separate for me now.

I move forward in peace and joy, love and harmony.
I move forward in _____.

151

Clearing – Twelve Steps

This script is an adaptation of the twelve steps followed by Alcoholics Anonymous. It can be used for any addiction — alcohol, drugs, cigarettes, food, work, relationships, sports, shopping, etc. Modify it to fit your personal situation and philosophical beliefs. If you haven't recorded the *Self Esteem* and/or *Personal Power* Scripts, you might add them here.

Addiction and I are one.
I now release and forgive myself for being addicted
*   to _____.*
I now release and forgive myself for not being addicted
*   to _____.*
I now transcend addiction.
I release and forgive _____ for being addicted and modeling
*   addiction to me.*
I release and forgive society for being addicted.
I release and forgive institutions for being addicted.
I release and forgive _____ for being addicted.
I now dissolve all family messages around addiction as
*   appropriate.*
I now dissolve all societal messages around addiction as
*   appropriate.*
I now dissolve all religious messages around addiction as
*   appropriate.*
I now dissolve all _____ messages around addiction as
*   appropriate.*
I now dissolve all addiction patterns from my mind.
I now dissolve all addiction patterns from my body.
I now dissolve all addiction patterns from my emotions.
I now dissolve all addiction patterns from my spirit.

Denial and I are one.
I release and forgive myself for denying my addiction.
I admit and acknowledge my addiction.
I am honest with myself about my addiction.
I am honest with myself about my past — who I have been and
*   what I have done.*
I now transcend denial.

153

I am safe and protected when I acknowledge my addiction.
I am loved and accepted when I acknowledge my addiction.
I am strong and courageous when I acknowledge my addiction.
Acknowledging my addiction has all positive outcomes for me
    now.

I acknowledge my life has become unmanageable.
I know a higher power can restore me to wholeness and health.
I know a higher power can restore me to sanity.
I surrender my will and my life to that higher power.
I trust the higher power to guide me through the process to a
    life of honor and integrity.
I trust the higher power to guide me through the process to a
    life of _____.

I now make an honest and complete self-inventory of who I am.
I now make a searching and courageous inventory of the way I
    live.
I admit the exact nature of my wrongs to myself.
I admit the exact nature of my wrongs to a higher power.
I admit the exact nature of my wrongs to another person as
    appropriate.

I release and forgive myself for these wrongs.
I know the higher power releases and forgives me for these
    wrongs.
I am ready to live free of my shortcomings.
I am entirely ready to have the higher power remove those
    wrongs.
I humbly ask the higher power to remove my shortcomings.
I release my shortcomings completely.
I transcend my shortcomings completely.

I identify all persons I have harmed as appropriate.
I release and forgive myself for harming others.
I release and forgive myself for harming _____.
I transcend harming others.
I make direct amends to all persons I have harmed as
    appropriate.
I am at peace with the people I have harmed.

I know the higher power forgives me for harming others.

Being wrong has no power over me.
I know when I am wrong and I admit it openly.
I share who I am with others at all appropriate times.
I share who I am with others in all appropriate ways.

I improve my conscious contact with higher power daily.
My feeling of oneness with the higher power increases daily.
I pray and meditate regularly.
I pray and meditate for the appropriate things.
I pray and meditate for the power to live for higher purpose.

I am one with these principles.
I practice these principles in my daily life.
I live these principles, and it shows.
I live in peace and harmony.
I live in love and forgiveness.
I live in clarity and honesty.
I live in health and balance.
I live in _____.
I live my higher purpose daily.

9

Affirmation Scripts

Action and Completion

The emptying-the-cup script:

Procrastination and I are one.
I now release and forgive myself for procrastinating.
I now release and forgive myself for not procrastinating.
I now transcend procrastinating.
I release and forgive _____ for modeling procrastination
*   to me.*
Completion and I are one.
I now release and forgive myself for not completing.
I now release and forgive myself for completing.
I now transcend completing.

The filling-the-cup script:

Appropriate action and I are one.
I direct my energy toward action.
I focus my energy on action.
I control and channel my energy into action.
I channel my energy in all positive ways.
I transform thoughts and feelings into action when
*   appropriate.*
I recognize effective action instantly and I take it.
I recognize when to move to action and I do it.
I am safe and protected when I take action.
I am accepted and acknowledged when I take action.
I am loved and nurtured when I take action.
I am sensible and practical when I take action.
I am free and spontaneous when I take action.
I accept my actions completely, even when they need
*   modification.*
I am willing to try new actions.
I focus on my actions that have worked.
I learn from my actions that have not worked.
It is easy for me to direct my motivation and energy to
*   actions that work.*
I focus on the task at hand.
I stay on track to accomplish _____.
I am safe and protected when I stay on track.
I am loved and nurtured when I stay on track.

161

I am exciting and adventurous when I stay on track.
I am sensible and practical when I stay on track.
I am at peace and joyful when I stay on track.
I focus through completion.
I complete in peace and harmony.
Completion and peace are one for me.
I am safe and protected when I complete.
I am accepted and acknowledged when I complete.
I provide value when I complete.
I am well rewarded on many levels when I take action.
I am well rewarded on many levels when I stay on task.
I am well rewarded on many levels when I complete.
I am appropriate action.
I am focus.
I am completion.

Assertiveness

The emptying-the-cup script

Assertiveness and I are one.
I now release and forgive myself for being assertive.
I now release and forgive myself for not being assertive.
I now transcend being assertive.
I release and forgive _____ for not teaching me to be assertive.
I release and forgive _____ for not modeling assertiveness to me.
Setting limits and I are one.
I release and forgive myself for setting limits.
I release and forgive myself for not setting limits.
I now transcend setting limits.
I release and forgive _____ for not teaching me to set limits.
I release and forgive _____ for not honoring my limits.
I release and forgive _____ for not modeling setting limits to me.
Saying no and I are one.
I release and forgive myself for saying no.
I release and forgive myself for not saying no.
I now transcend saying no.
Saying no and feeling guilty are separate for me now.
Setting limits and feeling guilty are separate for me now.
Being assertive and feeling guilty are separate for me now.
Being assertive and feeling defensive are separate for me now.
Being assertive and feeling _____ are separate for me now.
Being assertive and being healthy are the same for me now.
Being assertive and being _____ are the same for me now.

The filling-the-cup script

It is natural for me to be assertive.
I am safe and protected when I am assertive.
I am loved and accepted when I am assertive.
I am supported and nurtured when I am assertive.

163

I feel good when I am assertive.
I am gracious when I am assertive.
I am natural and smooth when I am assertive.
I am spontaneous and free when I am assertive.
I am joyful and happy when I am assertive.
I am proud of myself when I am assertive.
I am _____ when I am assertive.
I am assertive when appropriate.
I am assertive at all appropriate times in all appropriate
*   ways.*
I say what I mean and I mean what I say.
I acknowledge my own thoughts and feelings.
I am assertive about my thoughts and feelings.
I enjoy being honest and asking for what I want and need.
I ask for what I want and need simply and clearly.
I ask for what I want and need firmly and smoothly.
I ask for what I want and need with ease and grace.
I ask for what I want and need in joy and peace.
I ask for what I want and need _____
I am safe and protected when I ask for what I want and need.
I am loved and accepted when I ask for what I want and need.
I am _____ when I ask for what I want and need.
I bring discussions about what I want and need to
*   completion with ease.*
I bring discussions about what I want and need to
*   completion in peace.*
I tell others what I want and need from them.
I tell others what I expect from them.
I monitor what I receive in relation to what I ask for.
I give appropriate feedback when I get what I ask for.
I give appropriate feedback when I don't get what I ask for.
I manage my relationships based on how they meet my wants
*   and needs.*
I maintain open, honest relationships.
I maintain relationships that support my assertiveness.
I maintain relationships that honor my limits.
I feel good about myself when I am assertive and set limits.
I increase in assertiveness daily.
I am assertive.

Change

The emptying-the-cup script:
Change and I are one.
I now release and forgive myself for changing.
I now release and forgive myself for not changing.
I release and forgive _____ for teaching me to fear change.
I release and forgive _____ for modeling resistance to change.
I now release and forgive the changes in my life.
I now transcend change.

The filling-the-cup script:
Change is the natural law of my life.
I choose to change.
I want to change.
I welcome change.
I change easily and effortlessly now.
I release and dissolve all patterns that prevent change.
I release and dissolve all patterns that prevent growth.
I release and dissolve all patterns that prevent transition.
I make positive changes daily.
Changing my thoughts makes me feel good.
Changing my habits makes me feel good.
Changing my actions makes me feel good.
My thoughts are changing in all appropriate ways.
My thoughts are all positive now.
My new world is a reflection of my new thinking.
I see the positive in every situation.
I see the positive in every transition.
I see the gift each change in my life has for me.
I trust life's process to bring me my highest good.
Everything is working for my highest good now.
Whatever I need comes to me.
Whatever I need to know is revealed to me.
My next step is clear to me now.
I am on path.
It is a joy to plant new seeds for the future.
It is a delight to embark on new directions.

It is fun to make new beginnings.
My life is ever new.
Each moment of my new life is fresh and vital.
My situation improves daily.
I move to the new with ease and joy.
I am at peace with being out of control.
I am safe and protected whether or not I am in control.
I am loved and accepted whether or not I am in control.
I am nurtured and supported whether or not I am in control.
I am spontaneous and joyful whether or not I am in control.
I am in grace whether or not I am in control.
I see life as a process, ever unfolding.
I appreciate each stage of the unfolding.
I enjoy each new development in the process.
I take joy in becoming.
I am ever new.
I accept my new situation with ease.
I accept my changing situation with dignity.
I accept these conditions with peace.
I accept each stage of my transition as appropriate.
I accept each phase of my life as natural.
I am different, while I am the same.
I am constant, while I am changing.
I am secure, while I am changing.
I am safe, while I am changing.
I enjoy the change process itself.
I face my unknown future with peace.
I face my unknown future with security .
I face my unknown future wise, free, and unafraid.

I put this situation in the hands of infinite love and wisdom. If this is divine plan, I bless it and accept it. If it is not divinely planned, I give thanks that it is now dissolved and dissipated (Florence Scovel Shinn, *The Game of Life and How to Play It*).

Clearing and Completing

The emptying-the-cup script:

Completion and I are one.
My completion techniques and I are one.
I now release and forgive _____'s completion techniques.
I now release and forgive _____ for not completing.
I now release and forgive my completion techniques.
I now release and forgive myself for completing.
I now release and forgive myself for not completing.
I now release and forgive myself for not completing _____.
I now release and forgive myself for not completing
*   with _____.*
I now release and forgive _____ for not completing
*   with me.*
I now release and forgive _____ for not teaching me
*   completion.*
I now transcend my completion techniques.
I now transcend completion.
Clearing and I are one.
My clearing techniques and I are one.
I now release my clearing/completion techniques as
*   appropriate.*
I now release and forgive my clearing techniques.
I now release and forgive _____ for not clearing with me.
I now release and forgive myself for not clearing with _____.
I now transcend my clearing techniques.
I now release and forgive _____ for not teaching me
*   clearing techniques.*
I now transcend clearing.

The filling-the-cup script:

I recognize and honor my clearing techniques.
I now incorporate my past clearing/completion techniques
*   into my present as appropriate.*
I develop future clearing/completion techniques as
*   appropriate.*
I recognize the most appropriate clearing/completion
*   techniques for each situation.*

I use the most appropriate clearing/completion techniques for each situation.

I use what works and release all else in peace and love.

Clearing and completing have all positive outcomes for me now.

I am safe and protected when I clear and complete.

I am loved and accepted when I clear and complete.

I am supported and nurtured when I clear and complete.

I am happy and healthy when I clear and complete.

I am _____ when I clear and complete.

I clear and complete for my highest good.

I clear and complete in peace and love.

I clear and complete in harmony and joy.

I clear and complete in health and happiness.

I clear and complete in _____.

I am clear.

I am complete.

Confidentiality

The emptying-the-cup script:

Confidentiality and I are one.
I release and forgive myself for handling information well.
I release and forgive myself for not handling information well.
I release and forgive myself for breaking_____'s confidence.
I release and forgive _____ for breaking my confidence.
I transcend confidentiality.

The filling-the-cup script:

I understand the power of information.
I am safe and secure with my power.
I am safe and secure with information.
I maintain clarity around information issues.
I clear information in all appropriate ways.
I am at peace with information.
I give and receive information in all appropriate ways.
I balance my need to express with the need for confidentiality.
I balance my freedom and independence with the need for confidentiality.
All of my expression needs are met in all appropriate ways.
I am safe and at peace with my expression issues.
I am in harmony with my expression issues and needs.
Discretion and I are one.
I am at peace with discretion issues.
I feel good when I am discreet.
I feel powerful when I am discreet.
I feel loved, accepted, and acknowledged when I am discreet.
I am discreet with information when appropriate.
I am safe and at peace with authority.
I am safe and at peace being authority.
I am discretion.
I am confidentiality.

169

Consciousness

The emptying-the-cup script:

Being conscious and I are one.
I now release and forgive my family for not being fully conscious.
I now release and forgive _____ for not being fully conscious.
I now release and forgive myself for being conscious.
I now release and forgive myself for not being conscious.
I now transcend being conscious.

The filling-the-cup script:

I now choose to be fully conscious.
I now choose to be fully conscious mentally.
I now choose to be fully conscious physically.
I now choose to be fully conscious emotionally.
I now choose to be fully conscious spiritually.
I now choose to be fully conscious about _____.
I dissolve anything that prevents my functioning fully consciously in my personal relationships.
I dissolve anything that prevents my functioning fully consciously in my business relationships.
I dissolve anything that prevents my functioning fully consciously in _____.
I am safe and protected when I'm fully conscious.
I am loved and accepted when I'm fully conscious.
I am nurtured and acknowledged when I'm fully conscious.
I am spontaneous and free when I'm fully conscious.
I am joyful when I'm fully conscious as appropriate.
I am _____ when I'm fully conscious.
I am conscious of who I am and what I do.
I am conscious of what I create in my life.
I am conscious of my thoughts and the power of my thoughts.
I am conscious of my feelings and the power of my feelings.
I stay conscious in my relationships.
I stay conscious in my work.
I stay conscious _____.

I am conscious of the signals I send out.
I am conscious of the power of the signals I send out.
I process consciously in all appropriate ways.
I process consciously in all joyful ways.
I process consciously in all peaceful ways.
Consciousness and I are one.
I am consciousness.

Control

The emptying-the-cup script:
Control and I are one.
I now release and forgive _____ for controlling me.
I now release and forgive_____ for not controlling me.
I now release and forgive myself for being controlled.
I now release and forgive myself for letting others control me.
I now release and forgive myself for not letting others control me.
I now release and forgive myself for controlling myself.
I now release and forgive myself for not controlling myself.
I now release and forgive myself for being controlling.
I now release and forgive myself for controlling others.
I now release and forgive myself for controlling _____.
I now transcend control and my control issues.
Letting go and I are one.
I now release and forgive myself for not letting go.
I now release and forgive myself for not letting go of _____.
I now release and forgive _____ for not letting go of me.
I now release and forgive myself for letting go.
I now transcend letting go.

The filling-the-cup script:
I am in control of my time and my life.
I am safe and secure whether or not I am in control.
I am loved and accepted whether or not I am in control.
I am honored and acknowledged whether or not I am in control.
I am happy and free whether or not I am in control.
I am joyful and spontaneous whether or not I am in control.
I am successful and productive whether or not I am in control.
I am provided for and taken care of whether or not I am in control.
I am in charge whether or not I am in control.
I am _____ whether or not I am in control.
Control and power are separate for me now.

Controlling others and feeling powerful are separate for
   me now.
I choose when to control and when to release.
I always control the right things at the right times.
I always release the right things at the right times.
I balance control and release perfectly.
I control when appropriate.
I release when appropriate.
I am now willing to let go.
I am now willing to let go of _____.
I choose when to let go and when to hold on.
I always let go of the right things at the right times.
I always hold on to the right things at the right times.
I let go as appropriate.
I hold on as appropriate.
I am safe and protected when I let go.
I am loved and acknowledged when I let go.
I am happy and free when I let go.
I am nurtured and supported when I let go.
I am successful and productive when I let go.
I am _____ when I let go.
All of my issues around control, release, and letting go are
   now dissolved.

Decision Making
and Problem Solving

The emptying-the-cup script:
Decision making and I are one.
I now release and forgive _____ for making decisions.
I now release and forgive _____ for not making decisions.
I now release and forgive _____ for being the decision maker.
I now release and forgive myself for making decisions.
I now release and forgive myself for not making decisions.
I now transcend decision making.
Problem solving and I are one.
I now release and forgive my problems.
I now release and forgive _____ for having problems.
I now release and forgive _____ for not solving problems.
I now release and forgive myself for having problems.
I now release and forgive myself for not having problems.
I now release and forgive _____ for creating problems for me.
I now release and forgive myself for creating problems.
I now release and forgive myself for not creating problems.
I now release and forgive myself for solving problems.
I now release and forgive myself for not solving problems.
I now transcend having problems, creating problems, and problem solving.

The filling-the-cup script:
I now choose to be fully conscious about _____.
I approach the situation with peace and calm.
I am clear on my objectives in the situation.
I see my personal issues and how they affect my perspective.
I separate my personal issues from the situation as appropriate.
I integrate my personal philosophy into the decision making.
I see all sides of the issues as appropriate.
I think creatively about the situation and the possible solutions.

I identify various approaches to solving the situation with ease.
I recognize various solutions for each approach effortlessly.
I identify the possible outcomes for each approach and for each solution.
I analyze the outcomes in relation to my objectives.
I place the outcomes in perspective easily and effortlessly.
I have an innate sense of timing in the situation.
I choose when to act and when to react.
I do all the right things at the right times.
I succeed in solving each situation in grace and abundance.
I am shown exactly what to do, under all circumstances and in all places.
I know everything I need to know now.
I express wisdom and understanding and make the right decisions quickly.
I maintain peace and calm while I make decisions.
I am spontaneous and free when I make decisions.
I am safe and protected when I make decisions.
I am loved and accepted when I make decisions.
I am supported and acknowledged when I make decisions.
I make decisions for myself as appropriate.
I make decisions for others as appropriate.
I know when to make decisions and when to flow.
I am guided to perfect outcomes.
Making decisions has all positive outcomes for me now.

Financial Planning

The emptying-the-cup script:
Financial planning and I are one.
I now release and forgive myself for doing financial planning.
I now release and forgive myself for not doing financial planning.
I now release and forgive _____ for not teaching me financial planning.
I now transcend financial planning.

The filling-the-cup script:
I assume the responsibility for my financial plans.
I enjoy making my financial plans.
It is fun for me to plan my money matters.
I am a good money manager.
I have specific financial goals.
I have a written financial plan to achieve those goals.
I have a twenty year goal.
I have a ten year goal.
I have a five year goal.
I have yearly goals.
I write short range plans to fit my goals.
Before I spend money, I consider my goals.
I see my money as a positive and powerful tool.
I am good at making and saving money.
I enjoy receiving money for a job well done.
I give and receive value equally.
I make more than I spend.
I am good at managing my money.
I make wise investments.
My net worth increases each month.
I am reaching my financial goals easily.
I have a realistic monthly budget.
Before I spend money, I consider my budget.
I stay within my budget easily.
I save money regularly each month.
I pay myself first.

I know where I stand financially every day.
I keep my financial records accurate and up to date.
I balance my checkbook easily.
When it comes to money, I am in control.
I understand my taxes.
I understand tax saving investments.
I have excellent banking relationships.
I have sufficient protection through insurance.
My financial affairs and records are organized.
I continually review my estate planning.
I spend money on things that benefit me.
I invest in appreciating assets.
I'm good at analyzing investments.
I have good money sense and judgment.
Once a year, I check my credit rating.
Abundance is my natural state of being.
I have sufficient money for my personal use.
I deserve the best in life.
I give myself the best in life.
I have a healthy attitude about money.
I now have a financial success consciousness.
Money and I are one.
I am one with my money.
My money and I are good partners.

Focusing

The emptying-the-cup script:

Focusing and I are one.
I now release and forgive _____ for being focused.
I now release and forgive_____for not being focused.
I now release and forgive myself for being focused.
I now release and forgive myself for not being focused.
I now transcend focusing.

The filling-the-cup script:

I choose to focus when appropriate.
I am guided to focus when appropriate.
I am guided through the focusing process.
I move through the process with ease.
I process in all appropriate ways.
I am guided to focus when appropriate.
I am guided through the focusing process.
My mind leads me through how to focus effectively.
My emotions allow me to focus effectively.
I trust my body to work with me for focusing.
I trust my body to have the wisdom for focusing.
I welcome everything that comes from focusing.
I openly receive everything that comes from focusing.
I can leave focusing at will.
I can return to focusing at will.
I know when to stop and when to continue.
I continue through completion as appropriate.
I prepare appropriately.
I begin by getting comfortable.
I provide for my physical comfort.
I arrange my physical space to my liking.
I mentally and physically relax.
I put my attention in my body.
I let my body feel whole and sound.
I clear a mental space for focusing.
I choose the issue for focusing.
I am guided to select the most appropriate issue.
I distance myself from the issue.

I place the issue outside myself, at a distance.
I allow the feeling of this issue to float up.
I sense how this issue feels in my body.
I know what to pay attention to, and what to dissolve.
I continue until I feel the single feeling that encompasses all of the issue.
I recognize the feeling of this issue.
I acknowledge the feeling of the whole issue.
I identify the special quality of this issue for me.
I get words or pictures that embody the special quality.
I recognize its relationship to my past as appropriate.
I sense the significance of this issue.
I subtly shift to the core feeling of the issue, and I dissolve all else.
I experience a confirming sensation.
I experience a physical release.
I match my felt sense with my process.
I reject the familiar answers for fresh messages when appropriate.
I listen to the messages from my body.
I experience a sense of the whole issue.
I let the images flow out of my feelings.
I let my words flow out of my feelings.
I recognize what my felt sense needs from me.
I easily identify what is necessary for this to feel OK.
I expect positive changes and I get them.
I create positive changes and I feel it in all positive ways.
My body processes, changes, moves, and releases.
I feel good when I focus.
I focus with ease and in grace.
I feel good when I take care of myself in this way.
I feel safe being in control of my own process.
I experience change in all positive ways.
I am focusing.

(This is a specific technique developed by Eugene Gendlin. Listen to the tape awake to move you through the process. Listen to it asleep to teach your mind/brain the technique. Details are available in *Focusing*, by Eugene T. Gendlin, Bantam Books, 1978.)

Global Community

The emptying-the-cup script:
The global community and I are one.
I release and forgive myself for not being part of the global community.
I release and forgive myself for being part of the global community.
I release and forgive the global community for _____.
I now transcend the global community.
Global issues and I are one.
I now transcend global issues.

The filling-the-cup script:
It is appropriate for me to work with global issues.
It is appropriate for me to work on a global level.
I am safe and protected when I work on a global level.
I am supported and nurtured when I work on a global level.
I am acknowledged and appreciated when I work on a global level.
Global resources and I are one.
My gifts and abilities are global in scope.
My role is global in scope.
My skills and abilities are global in scope.
My future is global in scope.
I participate effectively in global experiences.
I provide value to others through global experiences.
International networking and I are one.
I recognize networking possibilities and I follow up on them.
I attract appropriate national contacts.
I attract appropriate international contacts.
I attract appropriate global leaders.
Cultural diversity and I are one.
I now transcend cultural diversity.
I now transcend global competition.
I now transcend global hatred and prejudice.
Global security and I are one.
Global economy and I are one.
Global peace and I are one.

I am naturally drawn to millennium concepts.
I am naturally drawn to millennium leaders and groups.
I am naturally drawn to millennium energies and guides.
I am naturally drawn to millennium systems and
  organizations.
I am naturally drawn to millennium techniques and
  matrixes.
I am global peace and love.
I am global joy and harmony.
I am global peace and equality.

Goal Setting

The emptying-the-cup script:

Goal setting and I are one.
I now release and forgive myself for not setting goals.
I now release and forgive myself for setting goals.
I now release and forgive _____ for not setting goals.
I now release and forgive _____ for being driven by goals.
I now transcend goal setting.

The filling-the-cup script:

I enjoy planning my life.
I take pleasure in setting balanced life goals.
It is fun for me to write goals for myself.
My goals are reasonable and reachable.
My goals are challenging.
My goals are well thought out.
My goals are balanced.
My goals promote my personal growth.
My goals promote my professional growth.
My goals promote my personal freedom.
My goals promote my professional freedom.
My goals promote my emotional and spiritual freedom.
My goals promote my financial freedom.
My goals are written.
*I have written goals in all areas of my life — personal and
    professional.*
I make detailed plans to achieve my goals.
I write down the steps to attain each goal.
*I make daily "to do" lists that include goal reaching
    activities.*
I enjoy taking the steps to achieve my goals.
I set aside time each day to review my goals.
I visualize my goals already achieved.
I focus on my goals.
I match my behavior to my goals.
*I allow myself to change or modify my goals when
    appropriate.*
I review and update my goals regularly.

My values are reflected in my goals.
I know what makes me happy, and that is reflected in my goals.
I live a balanced life, and that is reflected in my goals.
It is OK for me to have everything I want.
It is OK for me to succeed.
I take full responsibility for my life.
I accept full responsibility for my choices and my decisions.
I take pleasure in taking responsibility for myself.
I feel empowered when I write goals.
I feel powerful when I achieve my goals.
The process of achieving my goals is fun for me.
I am persistent in the pursuit of my goals.
It is easy for me to take the steps to achieve my goals.
It is easy for me to activate myself toward goal attainment.
It is fun for me to find solutions for goal attainment.
I have many talents, and I use them well.
I have sufficient time and energy to accomplish my goals.
I have a great attitude toward myself and my goals.
I know that life has endless opportunities for me.
I take pride in achieving.
I take pleasure in performing well.
It is fun to be activated toward my goals.
It is exciting to achieve my goals.
I am now creating my life exactly as I want it to be.
I am the artist of my own creation.
My creation is appropriate to my unique personality.
My goals are appropriate to my unique personality.
My goals are fun!

Healing: Christian

A filling-the-cup script:
I recognize God as the all encompassing Mind.
I recognize Christ as the all loving.
I recognize Spirit as the all active manifestation.
I am soul, I am body, and I am spirit, and the three are one.
The Kingdom of God is within me.
I am the vessel of God and I express God.
In God I live and move and express my feelings.
I am a tower of strength and stability in the realization that God is my health.
God and heaven and earth, and all the healing powers are united in healing me.
I press forward with courage and boldness in the power of God, and I am healed.
The peace of God wells up within me.
I trust in God in all things and I am obedient to God.
God lives in me now.
By the Grace of God, through Christ Jesus, I am made whole.
I welcome Christ into my body.
I recognize Christ as the embodiment of the God-Mind.
My mind is cleansed by Christ.
I have new life in Christ, and I am healed.
My new life in Christ fills me with zeal to live, and I am healed.
The Christ quickens and heals me.
Eternal life and strength are here, and I am made whole through Jesus Christ.
I am in unity with the Spirit of Truth
My life source is Spiritual energy.
I recognize Truth as it is in principle.
The Spirit of wholeness quickens me and heals me.
I am strengthened and healed by the power of the Spirit of the inner me.
I daily praise and thank the Spirit of Life and Health for constantly restoring me to perfection of body.

184

*I praise and give thanks that the strength and power of
  Spirit now restore me to harmony and health.*

*I have the power to release the divine life imprisoned in my
  cells and project is as spiritual energy.*

*The vitalizing energy floods my whole being, and I am
  healed.*

I rejoice because thy harmonizing love makes me whole.

My life flows swift and strong.

My soul bursts forth in song.

I will sing unto the Lord a new song of harmony and health.

I am one with Divine mind — serene, orderly, and placid.

I sow seeds of love and the joy of life.

I acknowledge fulfillment.

I amupright and honest in all that I think and do.

I do unto others as I would have them do unto me.

I have order in my physical life.

I have order in my mental life.

I have order in my emotional life.

I have order in my spiritual life.

I establish myself in the spiritual law.

I am the the offspring of God.

*I am one with His perfect wisdom which is now ordering my
  life in divine harmony and health.*

I affirm divine order daily.

My faith is constant and unchanging.

My word is the measure of my power.

I use my mind for right thinking.

My thoughts radiate with the speed of spiritual light.

I diligently seek God in all I do.

I mentally concentrate on a perfect body.

I focus all of my mental powers on a perfect body.

I pray daily.

I lift my mortal mind to the plane of spirit daily.

*All things are possible to me when I exercise spiritual power
  under divine law.*

I liberate my mind 's energies through daily prayer.

I create a spiritual aura through daily prayer.

*Through my prayers, I adjust my mind and body in harmony
  with God's creative laws.*

I pray from a still place within myself.
I am persistent in prayer.
I am one with pure Being.
I am immersed in the Holy Spirit of life, love, and wisdom.
The law of perfect harmony and I are one.
I am open to learn Truth.
I am unlimited in my power.
I increase daily in health and strength, life and love.
I increase daily in wisdom and boldness, freedom and
*   charity.*
I am now in harmony with the Father, and stronger than any
*   mortal law.*
I know my birthright in pure Being, and I boldly assert my
*   perfect freedom.*
I am dignified and definite, yet meek in all that I think and
*   do.*
I am one with and I now fully manifest vigorous life,
*   wisdom, and spiritual understanding.*
I am one with and I now fully manifest love, charity, justice,
*   kindness, and generosity.*
I am one with and I now fully manifest infinite goodness and
*   mercy.*
Peace floweth through me like a river through my mind, and
*   I thank thee O God.*
I am body, I am soul, I am spirit — and these three are one.
I rejoice daily in my healing.
Healing and I are one.
I am healed.
I am.

(This script was taken from the book, *Jesus Christ Heals* by Charles Fillmore, Unity School of Christianity, Unity Village, Unity, MO, Copyright 1939.)

Health and Healing: General

The emptying-the-cup script:
Health and I are one.
I release and forgive myself for not being healthy.
I release and forgive myself for being healthy.
I release and forgive _____ for telling me I'm not healthy.
I release and forgive _____ for not being healthy.
I now transcend being healthy.

The filling-the-cup script:
I choose health.
I make the decisions daily that add to my good health.
My body is in balance, in perfect harmony with the universe.
I am strong and in perfect condition.
I am vibrantly healthy.
I love life.
I give thanks for my increasing health and vitality.
I am full of radiant health and energy.
Everything I do adds to my beauty and health.
I grow stronger and more powerful every day.
I take good care of myself every day.
I give my body the rest it needs.
I maintain a healthy balance of diet and exercise.
I sleep deeply, peacefully, and restfully.
I awaken invigorated and refreshed.
I eat what is best for my health.
I eat healthy food every day.
I eat fresh vegetables and fruits daily.
I eat whole grains daily.
My food is naturally salty.
Water is my favorite fitness drink.
I only eat when I'm hungry.
I eat slowly and chew each bite thoroughly.
I am full of energy and vitality.
Good health is natural to me.
I exercise in some form every day.
I exercise vigorously at least three times a week.
I enjoy walking as an exercise.

I have good stamina and endurance.
I am limber and agile.
My muscles are strong and flexible.
I schedule my exercise time and I stick to my schedule.
I enjoy working my body and feeling it perform.
My body is a powerful vehicle for my self expression.
Energy flows through my body easily.
Oxygen flows through my body easily.
Blood circulates through my body efficiently.
I breathe fully and freely.
I breathe deeply.
I love to breathe down into my abdomen.
The more I breathe, the more I live.
I think healthy thoughts as I breathe.
I see myself healthy.
I focus on health.
Good health and I are one.
I am adding years to my life.
I am youthing in mind.
I am youthing in body.
I am youthing in spirit.

Healing and I are one.
I take full responsibility for my healing.
My full healing and I are one.
I recognize my body signals.
I honor my body signals and I act on them.
I balance my physical, emotional, and mental bodies.
I recognize signals from each of these bodies as valid.
I listen to these body signals and I make changes
   accordingly.
I care about myself and my body.
I respect my life energy.
Life and I are one.
I live life fully and completely.
I experience joy daily.
I laugh easily and often.
I laugh deeply and fully.
I love to laugh.

My thoughts are positive about my healing.
Strength and health are my natural birthright.
I face my situation with optimism and enthusiasm.
I acknowledge miracles in my life daily.
I am excited about the miracle of my own healing.
I experience a sense of well being and inner peace.
I am always deeply centered and relaxed.
I attract the necessary support for my healing.
I see my body as well.
I visualize my own healing.
I see my inner body and body channels as clear.
I see my _____ healed.
My immune system is functioning properly.
My immune system operates more effectively every day.
My thalmus is balanced and active.
My white blood cells are activated and efficient.
My heart is open and clear.
My heart is charged with blood flow continually.
My liver is operating effectively.
My kidneys work efficiently.
My stomach and intestinal tract are balanced and healthy.
My reproductive organs are clear and open.
My mind is sending health signals to my entire body.
My brain is directing my cellular structures to increasing
    health.
My acid-base balance remains healthy for me.
I am drawn to the sources of health and healing for myself.
I am naturally attracted to those things that heal me.
I heal myself naturally every day.
I choose health and healing environments.
I choose health and healing habits.
I choose health and healing thoughts.
Good health and I are one.
Natural healing and I are one.
My healthy body and I are one.
Through right thinking, I bring right action.
I am mental healing.
Mental healing and I are one.
I am safe when I use mental healing.

I am loved and accepted when I use mental healing.
I am natural and normal when I use mental healing.
My mind is the seat of perfection for my body.
My faith-mind creates healing instantly and spontaneously.
My mind transforms ideas of health into my perfect physical condition.
My mind transforms images of health into my perfect physical condition.
My mind transforms feelings of health into my perfect physical condition.
I use my mind-energy to restore and illumine my body.
I transform the cells and tissues of my body with my mind.
I use my mind-energy to establish a lasting consciousness of mastery.
My faith/electricity is the base of my unlimited health.
My faith/electricity is the base of my permanent health.
I use my electrical impulses naturally.
My electrical impulses establish their primal equipoise effortlessly.
My supermind and I are one.
Supermind vitality and I are one.
I control my perfect health with my perfect supermind.
My supermind and I are one.
I am my supermind.

Holograms and Synergy

A filling-the-cup script:
Holograms and I are one.
I am a hologram of love and joy.
I am a hologram of abundance and prosperity.
I am a hologram of giving and receiving.
I am a hologram of nurturing and support.
I am a hologram of freedom and joy.
I am a hologram of commitment and consistency.
I am a hologram of harmony.
I am a hologram of light and illumination.
I am a hologram of world peace.
I am a hologram of _____.
Synergy and I are one.
I love and live synergistically.
I share energy synergistically.

Integrity and Ethics

The emptying-the-cup script:

Integrity and I are one.
I now release and forgive myself for having integrity.
I now release and forgive myself for not having integrity.
I now release and forgive _____ for not having integrity.
I now transcend integrity.

The filling-the-cup script:

I easily recognize integrity issues.
I see integrity issues clearly.
I maintain a balanced perspective with integrity issues easily.
I choose to be fully conscious about my personal integrity issues.
I transcend my family as the source of my integrity.
I transcend my community as the source of my integrity.
I transcend my society as the source of my integrity.
Authority and I are one.
I recognize universal source as the source of all integrity.
I recognize _____ as the source of my integrity.
My spirituality is the base of my personal integrity.
I balance my personal integrity with my professional decisions effortlessly.
It is easy for me to stand up for what I believe to be right.
I make decisions naturally, knowing my integrity is a given.
I am at peace with integrity and with integrity issues.
I feel good making integrity decisions.
I am calm and relaxed when I face integrity issues.
I am centered and balanced when I consider integrity issues.
It is easy for me to see what is ethical and what is not.
My standards of ethics are personal and individual.
My standards of ethics are universal.
I flow completely with what is ethical.
I am ethics.
I am integrity.

Performing Well

The emptying-the-cup script:
Performing well and I are one.
I now release and forgive myself for performing well.
I now release and forgive myself for not performing well.
I now release and forgive _____ for criticizing my performance.
I now transcend performing well.

The filling-the-cup script:
I am responsible for my performance.
I take full responsibility for what I do.
I enjoy knowing I am responsible for my actions.
I take pleasure in motivating myself.
I am reasonable in the performance level I expect of myself.
I know I can succeed and perform well.
I accept myself as imperfect and exceptional at the same time.
I enjoy doing high quality work.
I consistently do high quality work.
I place great value on taking appropriate action.
Solving problems helps me learn and grow.
I keep my mind open and alert for creative solutions.
Solutions come to me easily.
I have a great attitude about my performance.
I look forward to my workday.
I give and receive emotional support at work.
I give and receive positive feedback about my performance.
I have many talents, and I use them well.
I am a competent _____ and I appear that way to others.
I attract positive opportunities to myself.
I attract positive people to work with me.
I enjoy programming my mind positively each day.
My horizons are constantly expanding.
I improve daily in attitude and abilities.
Each day, I nourish and improve my mind.
Each day, I nourish and improve my body.

193

Each day, I nourish and improve my spirit.
Life holds endless opportunities for me.
I have a satisfying job.
I love doing my work.
I give and receive value equally.
I have a success consciousness.
I believe in myself and my future.
What others have done, I can do.
I rise to new heights consistently.
I grow stronger with each new challenge.
I attract work that provides me with prosperity.
I am willing to be successful and happy.
Success has all positive outcomes for me now.
I choose success.
I am an achiever.
I apply myself to my tasks with ease.
I apply myself to my tasks with joy.
I take great pleasure in achieving with excellence.
I make excellence a part of my daily life.
I focus on excellence and what it means to me.
I am comfortable with excellence and all it brings.
I am safe with excellence and peak performance.
I am one with excellence and peak performance.
I choose excellence and peak performance for myself.

Personal Power

The emptying-the-cup script:
Personal power and I are one.
I now release and forgive myself for having personal power.
I now release and forgive myself for not having personal power.
I now release and forgive myself for using my personal power.
I now release and forgive myself for not using my personal power.
I now release and forgive _____ for taking my power.
I now release and forgive myself for giving my power away.
I now release and forgive myself for not giving my power away.
I release and forgive myself for confusing control with power.
I release and forgive myself for confusing money with power.
I release and forgive myself for confusing prestige with power.
I release and forgive myself for confusing education with power.
I release and forgive myself for confusing position with power.
I release and forgive myself for confusing excitement and drama with power.
I release and forgive myself for confusing _____ with power.
I now transcend personal power.
Dependence and I are one.
I now release and forgive myself for being dependent.
I now release and forgive myself for not being dependent.
I now release and forgive _____ for modeling dependence to me.
I now transcend dependence.
Being rescued and I are one.
I now release and forgive myself for wanting to be rescued.

I now release and forgive myself for not wanting to be rescued.

I now release and forgive _____ for rescuing me.

I now release and forgive _____ for not rescuing me.

I now release and forgive myself for confusing being rescued with being loved.

I now release and forgive myself for confusing being rescued with _____.

I now release and forgive myself for rescuing others.

I now release and forgive myself for not rescuing others.

I now release and forgive myself for confusing rescuing others with having personal power.

I now release and forgive myself for confusing rescuing others with giving or receiving love.

I now release and forgive myself for confusing rescuing others with _____.

I now dissolve all issues around rescuing and being rescued with my personal power.

I now transcend rescuing and being rescued.

The filling-the-cup script

Power and I are one.

Natural power and I are one.

Internal power and I are one.

I am safe and protected when I use my power.

I am loved and accepted when I use my power.

I am nurtured and supported when I use my power.

I am spontaneous and free when I use my power.

I am _____ when I use my power.

I use my power for good.

My power has all positive outcomes for me now.

As I increase in power, my relationships increase in power.

As I increase in power, my health increases.

As I increase in power, my joy increases.

As I increase in power, my self satisfaction increases.

As I increase in power, _____ increases.

My total wellness is the base of my personal power.

My ability to feel is the base of my personal power.

My ability to trust is the base of my personal power.

My ability to understand and acknowledge truth is the base of my personal power.

My self love and acceptance are the base of my personal power.

My openness and vulnerability are the base of my personal power.

My strength is the base of my personal power.

My inner peace is the base of my personal power.

My joy and love are the base of my personal power.

My harmony and balance are the base of my personal power.

My abundance and prosperity are the base of my personal power.

My giving and receiving are the base of my personal power.

My acceptance and flow are the base of my personal power.

My freedom is the base of my personal power.

My spirituality is the base of my spiritual power.

My _____ is the base of my spiritual power.

I deserve all the personal power I want.

I am at peace with having personal power and using it.

I am personal power.

Prosperity: Personal I

The emptying-the-cup script:

Prosperity and I are one.
I now release and forgive _____ for being prosperous.
I now release and forgive _____ for not being prosperous.
I now release and forgive myself for being prosperous.
I now release and forgive myself for not being prosperous.
I now transcend prosperity.
I now dissolve all barriers to total and perfect prosperity.
I dissolve all family issues around prosperity as appropriate.
I dissolve all societal issues around money as appropriate.
I am now willing to be fully conscious of my prosperity
    issues.
I program myself for prosperity, dissolving all else.
I now embrace and dissolve everything that blocks my
    prosperity mentally.
I now embrace and dissolve everything that blocks my
    prosperity physically.
I now embrace and dissolve everything that blocks my
    prosperity emotionally.
I now embrace and dissolve everything that blocks my
    prosperity spiritually.
Money addictions and I are one.
I now release and forgive money addictions.
I now release and forgive _____for having money addictions.
I now release and forgive our society for having money
    addictions.
I release and forgive myself for having money addictions.
I release and forgive myself for not having money
    addictions.
I now transcend money addictions.

The filling-the-cup script:

I choose to be prosperous.
I am filled with prosperity thinking.
I deserve to be prosperous and wealthy.
I am responsible for creating prosperity in my life.
I am responsible for creating abundance in my life.

I recognize there are infinite resources in the universe.
I draw upon those unlimited resources for my own
  enrichment.
I have faith in my future and my destiny.
My creative mind creates my wealth.
What others have done, I can do.
I attract prosperity in many forms.
Divine source is my unending supply.
I recognize money as a form of energy.
I attract positive energy, and I circulate positive energy.
I circulate money in all positive ways.
I circulate money in all appropriate ways.
Spending money and being safe are separate for me now.
Spending money and being loved and accepted are separate
  for me now.
Spending money and being nurtured are separate for me
  now.
Spending money and having my needs met are separate for
  me now.
Spending money and loving and nurturing others are
  separate for me now.
Spending money and being in control are separate for me
  now.
Spending money and _____are separate for me now.
I am safe, loved, and accepted when I save money.
I am safe, loved, and accepted when I take care of myself.
I share my prosperity in all appropriate ways.
I share my material wealth in all appropriate ways.
Large sums of money come to me under grace, in perfect
  ways.
Taking care of myself financially has all positive outcomes
  for me now.
Having large sums of money has all positive outcomes for
  me now.
Being prosperous and wealthy has all positive outcomes for
  me now.
I am abundance.
I am prosperity.

Prosperity: Personal II

A filling-the-cup script:
Prosperity and I are one.
I choose prosperity.
I choose prosperity mentally.
I choose prosperity physically.
I choose prosperity emotionally.
I choose prosperity spiritually.
I recognize Mother/Father God as the source of my supply.
There is no limit to my supply.
There is no limit to the sources of my supply.
My resources are as far reaching as the universe.
My supply comes from all points in the universe.
My supply comes through all avenues of life.
My supply is crowding upon me now.
I am open and receptive to my highest good now.
New channels of prosperity open to me daily.
My infinite intelligence makes contact with the source daily.
I thank the source for unlimited increase in mind, money,
   and substance.
I always have something to give.
I give richly and I receive richly.
I give consistently and open the way to receive consistently.
I give freely my tenth to Mother/Father God's work, and I
   reap a hundredfold.
I tithe my way to unlimited prosperity now.
I tithe in all appropriate amounts and all appropriate ways.
I am aware that as I give, it will be returned to me tenfold or
   more.
I have a right to deserve immediate prosperity.
I am ready to receive prosperity now.
I am ready to receive unlimited good now in all areas of my
   life.
I am receiving now.
I am receiving all the good and goods the universe has for
   me now.
I picture only good and I receive it.

200

I expect the best and I attract the best in every experience.
The law of mental attraction opens wide every channel of
supply.
I invite power and love into my life, and every need is met.
I take only the good from each experience, and release all
else.
I begin now to recognize another set of circumstances.
I am divinely guided to see beyond appearances.
My progress is swift and joyous.
I am living a happy, harmonious life now.
I am ready to be prosperous in all ways in my life.
I mentally accept and claim my highest good now.
My prosperity is omnipresent.
I give thanks for my prosperity.

(This script was adapted from the book, *Secret of Unlimited Prosperity* by Catherine Ponder, DeVorss & Co., Box 550, Marina Del Rey, CA 90291.)

Receiving and
Being Supported

The emptying-the-cup-script:
Receiving and I are one.
I release and forgive myself for receiving.
I release and forgive myself for not receiving.
I release and forgive _____ for not supporting me.
I release and forgive myself for being supported.
I release and forgive myself for not being supported.
I now transcend receiving and being supported.

The filling-the-cup script:
I am safe and protected when I receive.
I am loved and nurtured when I receive.
I am trusting when I am open to receive.
I feel powerful when I receive.
I feel spontaneous and free when I receive.
I am open to receiving from all sources as appropriate.
I trust the abundant universe to care for me at all times in
*   all ways.*
I deserve to be emotionally supported.
I deserve to be physically supported.
I deserve to be mentally supported.
I deserve to be spiritually supported.
I deserve to support myself, and I deserve to have others'
*   support me.*
Self support and nurturing and I are one.
I am now willing to be supported by my family.
I am now willing to be supported by my own nurturing
*   parent.*
I am now willing to be supported by my own inner free
*   child.*
I am now willing to be supported by friends.
I am now willing to be supported by intimates.
I am now willing to be supported by men.
I am now willing to be supported by women.
I am now willing to be supported by my supervisor/boss.

I am now willing to be supported by my peers.
I am now willing to be supported by my subordinates.
I am now willing to be supported by the business community.
I am now willing to be supported by corporate America.
I am now willing to be supported by _____.
I am open to receive love from many sources.
I am now willing to be supported by God/universal source.
I am open to receive support from many sources.
I am safe when I receive love and support from many sources.
I accept love and support from all sources as appropriate.
I recognize _____ as the source of my supply.
I accept the source of my supply as unlimited.
Unlimited love and I are one.
Unlimited abundance and prosperity and I are one.
Unlimited support and nurturing and I are one.
Unlimited freedom and joy and I are one.
Unlimited peace and harmony and I are one.
It is natural for me to receive unlimited abundance and prosperity.
It is natural for me to receive unlimited support and nurturing.
It is natural for me to receive unlimited freedom and joy.
It is natural for me to receive unlimited peace and harmony.
I am unlimited receiving.
I am unlimited support.

Relationships

The emptying-the-cup script:

Good relationships and I are one.

I now release and forgive myself for having good relationships.

I now release and forgive myself for not having good relationships.

I release and forgive my family for their relationship issues.

I release and forgive _____ for his/her relationship with me.

I now dissolve all past relationship issues as appropriate.

I now transcend good relationships.

The filling-the-cup script:

Every person is a golden link in my good.

I am attracting loving, satisfying relationships.

I am attracting loving people.

I am attracting creative people.

I am attracting powerful people.

I am attracting spiritual people.

I am attracting _____.

I love to love and be loved.

I now give and receive love freely.

All things are working together for good in my life.

I am ready for all my relationships to work.

I am strong and loving in my relationships.

I am a powerful person, and that power enhances my relationships.

My personal power has all positive outcomes in my relationships.

I am whole in myself.

I deserve love.

I deserve pleasure.

I have an unlimited capacity for loving relationships.

I have an unlimited capacity for fulfilling relationships.

I receive love from many sources.

I encounter love wherever I go.

I am always nourished in my relationships.

My relationships are loving and harmonious.
My relationships are equal.
My communication is clear and productive in my
     relationships.
It is natural for me to tell the truth.
It is easy for me to express my feelings.
It is easy for me to ask for what I want.
I treat _____ with kindness.
_____ and I work toward the highest good.
_____ and I get closer every day.
I give thanks for having _____ in my life.
I thank myself for my relationship with _____.
I make friends easily.
I easily attract appropriate people to myself.
I keep in touch with my friends regularly.
I touch the people I care about.
It is easy for me to express my feelings with touch.
I always show positive concern for others.
I listen to improve my understanding of others.
I am honest in my relationships.
I am trustworthy in my relationships.
I am a sensitive, caring individual.
I am friendly, enthusiastic, and open with others.
I am warm and real.
I am the kind of person people like to be with.
I treat everyone I meet with courtesy and respect.
I respect others and they respect me.
I am sincerely interested in others.
I am a good listener.
I am attentive when others talk to me.
I care about others' beliefs, ideas, and feelings.
I take the time to understand others.
I help people feel good about themselves.
I give recognition and encouragement to others.
I enjoy the company of other positive people.
I look for positive qualities in everyone I meet.
I reflect positive qualities back to them.
My best friends like themselves.
I spend time with people I respect and love.
I give my friends the best of myself.

205

I feel good about the people in my life.
I'm fair in my dealings with others.
I always work toward a win-win in my relationships.
My friendships are genuine and real.
I create a feeling of trust with others.
It is easy for me to establish rapport with others.
I enjoy building mutually enriching relationships.
I plan time for my relationships.
I nurture my relationships.
I enjoy my business relationships.
I listen carefully when people talk to me.
I use direct eye contact when appropriate.
I enjoy noticing details about people I work with.
I'm aware of body language messages from others.
I remember names effortlessly.
I remember faces easily.
I have harmonious relationships with my family.
I am my own person, and I interact with my family on that basis.
I allow each family member to be an individual.
I respect each person's uniqueness.
I honor each person for his/her own way of becoming.
I am at peace with _____.
I share understanding with each family member.
I spend quality time with each family member alone
I plan time with my family.
I enjoy the time I spend with my family.
I enjoy the time I spend with _____.
I am unique, and I allow others their uniqueness.
I touch my family often.
I hug each family member daily.
I tell each person I love them in words.
I tell each person I love them in many ways.
I receive love from my family members constantly.
I see the love in my family all of the time.
I am now ready for all of my family relationships to work.
I live in peace and harmony in all of my relationships.
I see my relationships clearly.
I am one with my relationships.

Relationships: Intimacy

If you record this as a couple, you can use "we" in place of "I".

Some couples co-record by alternating voices; one person says the first affirmation, and the other person follows with the next affirmation. Some couples speak at the same time, layering one voice over the other. Find what works for you.

Intimacy and I are one.
I release and forgive my parents for not being intimate with each other.
I release and forgive my parents for not being intimate with me.
I release and forgive my parents for not knowing how to be intimate.
I release and forgive my parents for not teaching me how to be intimate.
I now release and forgive _____ for not knowing how to be intimate.
I now release and forgive _____ for not being intimate with me.
I now release and forgive myself for being intimate with

_____.
I now release and forgive myself for not being intimate with_____.
I now release and forgive myself for not knowing how to be intimate.
I now dissolve all issues around being intimate.
I now dissolve all past conditioning around being intimate.
I now dissolve all past conditioning around giving and receiving love.
I now dissolve anything that is in the way of my ability to be close.
I now transcend intimacy.
I deserve to have intimacy and love in my life.
I am intimate with myself first.
I give love and intimacy as appropriate.
I am safe and protected when I give love and am intimate.
I am happy and healthy when I give love and am intimate.

I am spontaneous and free when I give love and am
   intimate.
I am open to receive intimacy and love.
I am safe and protected when I receive intimacy and love.
I am happy and healthy when I receive intimacy and love.
I am spontaneous and free when I receive intimacy and love.
I am natural and flowing when I receive intimacy and love.
I give and receive love and intimacy equally.
I appreciate the people in my life who give me love.
I appreciate the people in my life who are intimate with me.
I make conscious decisions about getting close.
I am now willing to be completely close to myself.
I am now willing to be completely close to someone else.
I recognize how my past scripting affects my relationship.
My partner and I are one.
I now release and forgive my partner.
I now release and forgive my partner for _____.
I now release and forgive myself for _____.
I now transcend my partner.
I am in charge of creating the experience I have in the
   relationship.
I flow with my rhythms in the relationship.
I flow with my partner's rhythms in the relationship.
I flow with the rhythms of the relationship.
I am now willing for our relationship to be about giving and
   receiving love.
I am now willing for our relationship to be about giving and
   receiving the highest possible positive energy.
I am now willing for our relationship to be about having fun
   and living fully.
I am now willing for our relationship to be
   about_____.
I am now willing to be completely close to my partner.
I now transcend being close to my partner.
I am now willing to be completely separate.
I am now willing to be completely separate from my partner.
I am willing to be totally independent and totally close.
Being close and being dependent are separate for me now.
Being close and losing myself are separate for me now.
Being separate and being lonely are different for me now.

Being autonomous and being lonely are separate for me now.

I give myself the freedom to be separate.

I am safe and loved when my partner is complete without me.

I am safe and loved when my partner has experiences and feelings without me.

I am safe and loved when my partner has a life separate from mine.

I provide the space for my partner to be separate from me.

I flow with being close, and I flow with being separate.

I maintain intimacy when I am close and when I am separate.

I am willing to take space to nurture myself as appropriate.

I am willing to take space to nurture the relationship as appropriate.

I give and take space as appropriate.

I am in touch with my expectations of the relationship.

I am at peace talking about my expectations of the relationship.

I am accepted and acknowledged when I discuss my expectations of the relationship.

I tell the truth about my expectations of the relationship.

Making agreements and I are one.

I now release and forgive _____ for not keeping agreements with me.

I now release and forgive myself for keeping my agreements.

I now release and forgive myself for not keeping my agreements.

I now transcend keeping agreements.

I am conscious of the agreements in the relationship.

I am open to negotiating the agreements in the relationship.

I only make the agreements I want to make in the relationship.

I make meaningful agreements and I keep them.

I carry my agreements to completion in peace and harmony.

I call my partner on unkept agreements in all appropriate ways.

Withdrawal and I are one.

I now release and forgive _____ for withdrawing from me.
I now release and forgive myself for withdrawing.
I now release and forgive myself for not withdrawing.
I now transcend withdrawing.
Projection and I are one.
I recognize and accept projection in the relationship.
I now release and forgive _____ for projecting onto me.
I now release and forgive myself for projecting onto _____.
I now transcend projection in the relationship.
I transform projection in the relationship.
I am at peace exploring problems in the relationship.
I flow with exploring problems in the relationship.
I explore problems non-judgmentally.
I am willing to take responsibility for the problems as appropriate.
I am willing to experience the problem.
I am safe and loved when I experience the problem.
I am nurtured and supported when I experience the problem.
I love and accept my partner while we explore problems.
I nurture and support my partner while we explore problems.
I communicate about the problem in all appropriate ways.
I separate money issues from power and control issues.
I separate money issues from equality and love issues.
I separate money issues from sensuous and sexual issues.
I release and forgive _____ for trying to control the relationship.
I release and forgive myself for trying to control the relationship.
My needs are met whether or not I control the relationship.
My needs are met whether or not I control the expectations.
My needs are met whether or not I control the agreements.
I now transcend control in the relationship.
I am free to experience and explore all feelings that come up in the relationship.
I am safe and loved when I experience all of my feelings.
I am accepted and acknowledged when I experience all of my feelings.

I am nurtured and supported when I experience all my feelings.

I deal with whatever comes up in all conscious ways.

I deal with whatever comes up in all healthy and healing ways.

I deal with whatever comes up in all spontaneous and free ways.

I deal with whatever comes up in all loving and nurturing ways.

It is easy for me to tell the truth in my relationship.

I am safe and loved when I tell the truth.

I am accepted and acknowledged when I tell the truth.

I get my needs met when I tell the truth.

I communicate what is in my heart with honesty and integrity.

It is easy for me to listen to the truth in my relationship.

I am safe and loved when I listen to the truth.

I am accepted and acknowledged when I listen to the truth.

I face the truth with courage and commitment.

I am willing to have the relationship be a key to my full development.

I am willing to have the relationship be a key to my partner's full development.

I support and nurture my own highest well-being in the relationship.

I support and nurture my partner's highest well-being in the relationship.

I am willing to be fully empowered in the relationship.

I am willing for my partner to be fully empowered in the relationship.

I realize everything that happens is perfect for my growth at that moment.

I have a clear, truthful, evolving relationship.

I grow toward being a source of love for myself and others daily.

My relationship increases my aliveness, radiance, and wholeness.

I go beyond my past limits in this relationship.

I move toward greater personal freedom daily in this relationship.

*I am willing to establish higher and higher levels of intimacy
    daily.*
Being intimate has all positive outcomes for me now.
Being intimate has all positive consequences for me now.
I have the courage to open to new levels of truth and love.
*I have the courage to embrace my male and female
    consciousness.*
I am at peace with my feminine side.
I am at peace with my masculine side.
My feminine side and masculine side are in balance.
I am now willing to experience complete sexual pleasure.
I am now willing to have a fully equal relationship sexually.
*I am willing to open to my full sexuality and express it in
    ways that support myself, my partner, and my
    relationship.*
I am safe and protected when I open to my partner sexually.
*I am loved and supported when I open to my partner
    sexually.*
*I am accepted and nurtured when I open to my partner
    sexually.*
*My relationship is an ongoing source of physical and mental
    growth.*
*My relationship is an ongoing source of emotional and
    spiritual growth.*
I support my partner's highest well being.
I support a clear, truthful, evolving relationship at all times.
*I choose intimacy, and I heal myself as I heal my
    relationship.*

(The ideas in this script were taken from the book *Centering and
the Art of Intimacy* by Gay Hendricks, Ph.D., and Kathryn
Hendricks, Ph.D. Prentice-Hall, c. 1985.)

Releasing and Forgiving

The emptying-the-cup script:
Releasing and I are one.
Forgiving and I are one.
I recognize when to release and forgive and I do it.
I release and forgive in complete faith and trust.
I release and forgive in complete love and peace.
I release and forgive everyone in my past.
I release and forgive everyone in my present.
I release all issues around _____.
Forgiving and approving are separate for me now.
Forgiving and condoning are separate for me now.
Forgiving and agreeing are separate for me now.
Forgiving and _____ are separate for me now.
I release and forgive myself for my past.
I release and forgive myself for my patterns.
I release and forgive myself for my habits.
I release and forgive myself for my actions.
I release and forgive myself for _____.
I release and forgive _____ for _____.
I release and forgive _____ to go to his/her highest good
    so I can go to mine.
I release and forgive _____ for not releasing and
    forgiving me.
I recognize healthy situations, and I release all else.
I recognize healthy relationships, and I release all else.
I recognize healthy actions, and I release all else.
I recognize healthy thoughts, and I release all else.
I recognize healthy _____, and I release all else.

The filling-the-cup script:
I am safe and protected when I release and forgive.
I am protected by my knowledge of the past.
I am protected by my understanding of the past.
I am protected by _____ when I release and forgive.
My past is now complete and resolved harmoniously.
The more I release, the lighter I feel.
The lighter I feel, the more love I experience.

I am now living my love.
I am now living a positive and forgiving life.

Sales Calls and Cold Calling

A filling-the-cup script

I am in control of my time and my life.

I make autonomous career decisions, and I do what is best for me.

I make appropriate career choices for myself at all times, and I am at peace with those choices.

I feel good about being responsible for my career decisions.

I know a sales career is valid and worthwhile.

I take pride in being a salesperson.

I provide a valuable service, and it appears that way to others.

My family recognizes the valuable business service I provide.

My friends recognize the valuable business service I provide.

Society recognizes the valuable business service I provide.

Mommy and I are one.

Daddy and I are one.

My family and I are one.

My family approves of me and approves of my sales career.

I approve of myself and of my sales career.

Sales and I are one, and self promotion and I are one.

I provide value with who I am.

I provide value with what I do.

I give and receive value equally.

I am guided to provide the right services to the right people at the right time.

All of my sales and prospecting actions are appropriate.

I feel good providing information to others about my product.

I provide information to others about my product in all appropriate ways.

It is natural for me to mix business with pleasure when appropriate.

It is natural for me to approach family and friends with my product.

Ethical self promotion and I are one.

I feel good when I promote myself.

I am safe and protected when I promote myself.
I am loved and accepted when I promote myself.
I am supported and nurtured when I promote myself.
I feel at home being visible and standing out.
I am safe and protected when I am visible and stand out.
I am loved and accepted when I am visible and stand out.
I am supported and nurtured when I am visible and stand out.
I feel good about being in sales and standing out as a salesperson.
Prospecting and selling is natural for me.
It is fun for me to prospect, present, and close.
I am safe and protected when I am prospecting, presenting, and closing.
I am loved and accepted when I am prospecting, presenting, and closing.
I am supported and nurtured when I am prospecting, presenting, and closing.
I meet new friends daily when I am prospecting, presenting, and closing.
I am emotionally capable of self promotion and prospecting: it is natural for me.
I balance my self promotional activities with respect for the needs and rights of others.
I am responsible for myself and my performance.
I feel good being responsible for myself and my performance.
I am competent in my field and I appear that way to others.
It is fun for me to learn about my field, and I learn more each day.
I feel good with my level of product knowledge.
I get personal satisfaction from doing my job well.
I get a feeling of great accomplishment from doing my job well.
I accept myself completely as I am, knowing I am improving daily.
I am now willing to feel good about myself all the time.
I feel wonderful receiving the monetary rewards of my business.

I feel wonderful receiving the emotional rewards of my business.

I recognize the balance of monetary and emotional rewards in selling my product.

I find emotional satisfaction in selling with sensitivity and empathy.

I find intellectual satisfaction in selling with knowledge and skill.

I find spiritual satisfaction in selling with ethics.

I feel good being in sales.

I am always deeply centered and relaxed about myself and my profession.

I am at peace with who I am and what I do.

I am full of dignity and respect for who I am and what I do.

I take pride and pleasure in my role as a professional salesperson.

I have a mature understanding of my profession, and I feel good about that.

It is easy for me to transcend my manager, mentor, trainer, and consultant's level of performance.

My mind is filled with miracle consciousness.

I see the possibilities of my profession daily.

What others have done, I can do.

My mind is filled with positive thoughts and positive thinking.

I see new opportunities for myself and my business daily.

I see how my product can benefit all types of people.

I enjoy having social involvement with individuals and groups.

I am comfortable with all types of people.

I am at home with the top economic and social levels of society.

I am equally comfortable with all levels of professional people.

I am consistent in my approach and my performance, regardless of the types of people I am with.

I am at home making presentations to all types of people.

I feel good presenting to one person, or to a group of people.

I am adequately prepared for my presentations.
I balance technique with human skills.
I balance information with emotion.
I balance realism and objectivity with emotion and feelings.
I balance organization and planning with action and results.
I am consistently assertive, using persuasion when
  appropriate.
I feel good asking for what I want.
I feel safe asking for what I need.
It is easy for me to ask for what I want and need.
It is natural for me to confront others in all appropriate
  ways.
It is natural for me to be forward, and to put myself
  forward.
It is OK for me to be perceived as forward.
I feel good when I am spontaneous.
I am safe and loved when I am spontaneous.
I am at home taking social and emotional risks.
I have complete trust that everything is working for my
  highest good now.
I am at peace with the intensity of my own emotions.
I let go and let it flow when appropriate.
I am at peace being public and self disclosing to others.
I feel good when I show my emotions.
I experience excitement daily and I show it.
I experience joy daily and I show it.
I am clear on my personal values.
I am clear on my professional values.
I deserve to have all the education, wealth, and status I
  want.
I deserve to have all the love, security, and peace I want.
I am safe and loved when I have education, wealth, and
  status.
I am safe and loved when I have security and peace.
I take joy in setting my career goals and achieving them.
I set goals that are achievable with who I am and where I am
  now.
My goals are well thought out and are specific.
I have a specific plan to achieve my goals.

I balance my goal planning with my action to achieve them.
I am a striver — a driver with a goal.
I see sales as the road to my wealth and status.
I see prospecting as the primary base for my sales.
I understand the prospecting cycle and I follow it well.
I have specific prospecting goals.
*I have a prospecting formula that works for me, and I stick
    to my formula as appropriate.*
*I know how many calls I want to make a day, and I make
    them easily and effortlessly.*
I have fun prospecting.
I choose to be fully conscious about prospecting.
I choose to be fully conscious when I am prospecting.
I make new friends and gather new information prospecting.
I feel good when I achieve my prospecting goals.
I find new ways to motivate myself to make my calls.
I make my prospecting calls at my best time of day.
I am on top of it when I do my prospecting.
*I keep accurate records of my prospecting which I enjoy
    reviewing.*
I am at home with prospecting.
I am at peace with prospecting.
I am safe and secure prospecting.
I am accepted and loved prospecting.
I am supported and nurtured prospecting.
I see prospecting as the pipeline to my unlimited wealth.

(This script is based on the findings in *The Psychology of
Call Reluctance,* Dudley and Goodson, Behavioral Science
Research Press, 1986.)

Self Esteem

The emptying-the-cup script:
Self esteem and I are one.
I now release and forgive myself for having self esteem.
I now release and forgive myself for not having self esteem.
I now release and forgive _____ for not giving me self esteem.
I now transcend self esteem.

The filling-the-cup script:
I take full responsibility for my self esteem.
I have a wonderful sense of who I am.
I take pleasure in my uniqueness.
I take pleasure in my commonness.
I am joyful with who I am and who I am becoming.
I treat myself with love all of the time.
I say positive things to myself and about myself.
I value and honor myself.
I respect my potential.
I enjoy being me.
I treat myself with respect.
I enjoy a loving relationship with myself.
I am independent and secure in my feelings.
I find value in all areas of my life.
I trust myself.
I like the person I see in the mirror every day.
I am a worthy person, aside from my accomplishments.
I am lovable and capable.
I am proud of being me.
I would rather be me than anyone else.
I see myself realistically and objectively.
I accept myself completely for who I am.
I give recognition and encouragement to myself.
I have many positive qualities.
I have many talents and abilities.
I'm a very interesting person.
I have a winning personality.
I am fun, friendly, and sincere.

I enjoy smiling, and I smile a lot.
I radiate positive, enthusiastic energy.
I am a happy person.
I find value in everything I do.
I find value in my life and life's purpose.
I take good care of myself.
I like what I do and I'm good at it.
I have a high degree of self worth.
I have a great deal of respect for myself.
I am a loving, nurturing parent to myself.
I am a carefree, playful child with myself.
My life is positive and fulfilling.
I trust myself.
I am my own person.
I love and approve of myself.
I appreciate all that I do.
I feel deep inner peace and serenity with my identity.
I have a keen sense of self identity.
I am secure in my identity.
I feel secure in all settings.
I feel my sense of identity in all settings.
I am a powerful, loving, creative being.
I am highly pleasing to myself in the presence of others.
I have a great deal to share with others.
All of my false images of myself from the past are now
    dissolved.
I have everything I need to enjoy the here and now.
I am lovable and I love myself.
I love and accept all of my feelings as part of myself.
I approve of myself without pleasing others.
I say no easily when appropriate.
It is safe for me to feel good about myself all the time.
I know what makes me happy and I do it.
I am getting more powerful every day.
Everything I need is within me.
I am the artist of my own creation.
I am filled with love and affection.
I have an unlimited capacity for enjoyment and pleasure.
I am joyous, happy and free.

I encounter love wherever I go.
I am a part of all I see and do.
I am a part of the Universe.
I am a part of everyone I meet.
I am whole and complete in myself.
I feel happy and blissful just being alive.
The Universe rejoices at my presence.
The Universe is glad I am here.
Self esteem and I are one.
I am self esteem.

Speaking: Public

The emptying-the-cup script:
Public speaking and I are one.
I now release and forgive myself for being a good public speaker.
I now release and forgive myself for not being a good public speaker.
I now release and forgive myself for being nervous when I speak.
I now release and forgive myself for not being nervous when I speak.
I now transcend public speaking.

The filling-the-cup script:
The audience and I are one.
I now transcend the audience.
I am safe and protected when I speak to groups.
I am loved and accepted when I share my ideas publicly.
I am supported and acknowledged when I discuss what I know.
I am spontaneous and free when I speak.
I balance my planning with my spontaneity speaking.
I use an outline and notes, and I speak naturally.
My words and ideas flow when I speak to groups.
I always say just the right thing at the right time.
My sense of timing is perfect.
I look forward to making public presentations.
I have fun when I share my ideas.
I smile a lot when I speak as appropriate.
I gesture effectively when I speak.
I am an effective speaker, and I appear that way to others.
I am a confident speaker, and I appear that way to others.
I am a powerful speaker in my own way, and I appear that way to others.
I stand erect and I speak clearly.
I am always deeply relaxed and calm.
My voice is even, forceful, and dynamic.
My hands are calm and quiet throughout my speech.

My breathing is deep and even throughout my speech.
I put emotion in my voice, and the audience responds well.
I speak from my heart as well as my head.
I maintain my head and heart connection while I speak.
I stay fully conscious while I speak.
I plan my presentation effectively.
I know my purpose for speaking and it shows.
I understand my material and it shows.
I know what I want from my audience, and I get it.
I know who my audience is, and I speak appropriately.
I match my presentation to my audience.
I get in tune with my audience right away and they feel it.
I create a bond of goodwill with my audience.
I flow with who they are, and they flow with who I am.
I have prepared visuals as appropriate.
I use my visuals perfectly.
I start with an attention getting opening.
I tell my audience what I'm going to tell them, then I tell
  them, then I tell them what I have told them.
I limit my number of main points as appropriate.
I cover the perfect amount of material for the time frame.
I help my audience understand the material.
I present the material in an interesting way.
I make the material relevant to the audience.
I use humor as appropriate.
I tell stories as appropriate.
My descriptions are visual and clear.
My definitions are clear and meaningful.
I am a natural storyteller and I enjoy it.
My audience enjoys the way I tell a story.
I sum up my talk when I am finished.
My summary is clear and concise.
I do a good job speaking, and I know it.
I get a good response to my presentation, and I am pleased.
I accept compliments about my speaking graciously.

Spirituality

Create this script to reflect your personal belief system.

The emptying-the-cup script:
Spirituality and I are one.
I now release and forgive myself for being spiritual.
I now release and forgive myself for not being spiritual.
I release and forgive _____ for not teaching me spirituality.
I release and forgive _____ for not modeling spirituality
  to me.
I now transcend spirituality.

The filling-the-cup script:
I am one with (God, The Goddess, Christ, Buddha, divine
  source, universal source, divine love, infinite intelligence,
  cosmic consciousness, etc.)
  _____is working through me now.
I am part of _____, and _____is part of me.
Divine love is creating miracles in my life daily.
Divine love is guiding me in all I do.
Divine love goes before me and prepares the way.
I am filled with divine light and love.
I am naturally enlightened.
I trust my inner knowing.
I am in tune with my higher self.
My higher self is guiding me in all I do.
My inner wisdom guides me.
My inner knowing is my most important source.
My mind and body now manifest divine perfection.
Divine order is now established in my mind and my body.
Divine order is now established in my relationships.
Every phase of my life is now in divine order.
Divine order heals and guides me.
I am one with divine plan.
I recognize divine plan.
I follow divine plan.
I am on path now.
I am fulfilling my perfect destiny.

225

The universe provides for me.
I draw on universal source for my supply.
The light of the eternal surrounds and protects me.
The white light surrounds and protects me at all times.
The Christ light surrounds and protects me.
I am filled with cosmic consciousness.
I feel the love and peace of the masters.
I grow toward oneness daily.
I maintain my spiritual balance daily.
I maintain my moral balance daily.
I maintain my soul balance daily.
I maintain my body as the temple of the living God.
I maintain my sacred trust easily and effortlessly.
My mind and body are in harmony with the eternal spirit.
I love myself: I love life: I love the Goddess.
I love myself: I love life: I love God.
I live my love daily.
I share my love daily.
I grow in spirit each day.
I grow in cosmic consciousness each day.
Everything in my world is perfect.
My mind is filled with miracle consciousness.
I choose miracles.
I acknowledge miracles.
I joyously let myself become a miracle in expression.

Success I

The emptying-the-cup script:
Success and I are one.
I now release and forgive _____ for being a success.
I now release and forgive _____ for not being a success.
I now release and forgive myself for being a success.
I now release and forgive myself for not being a success.
I now transcend success.
Male domination and I are one.
I now release and forgive male domination.
I now release and forgive the American society for being male dominated.
I now release and forgive business for being male dominated.
I now release and forgive government for being male dominated.
I now release and forgive the legal system for being male dominated.
I now release and forgive religion for being male dominated.
I now release and forgive education for being male dominated.
I now release and forgive _____ for being male dominated.
I now release and forgive (Dad) for dominating.
I now release and forgive (Mom) for being dominated.
I now release and forgive myself for being dominated.
I now release and forgive myself for not being dominated.
I now release and forgive the society for dominating me.
I now release and forgive the school system for dominating me.
I now release and forgive the church for dominating me.
I now release and forgive _____ for dominating me.
I now transcend male domination.
Female domination and I are one.
I now release and forgive female domination.
I now release and forgive _____ for being female dominated.
I now release and forgive _____ for dominating me.

227

I now release and forgive myself for being female dominated.

I now release and forgive myself for not being female dominated.

I now transcend female domination.

Giving away power and I are one.

I now release and forgive (Dad) for giving away his power.

I now release and forgive (Mom) for giving away her power.

I now release and forgive _____ for giving away his/her power.

I now release and forgive _____ for not giving away his/her power.

I now release and forgive myself for giving away my power.

I now release and forgive myself for not giving away my power.

I now transcend giving away power.

Independence and I are one.

I now release and forgive (Dad) for being independent.

I now release and forgive men for being independent.

I now release and forgive _____ for being independent.

I now release and forgive myself for being independent.

I now release and forgive myself for not being independent.

I now transcend being independent.

Dependence and I are one.

I now release and forgive (Mom) for being dependent.

I now release and forgive women for being dependent.

I now release and forgive _____ for being dependent.

I now release and forgive myself for being dependent.

I now release and forgive myself for not being dependent.

I now transcend dependence.

I balance my independence with my dependence.

I balance my independence with getting my needs met.

Female/male role models and I are one.

I now release and forgive all female/male role models as appropriate.

I now release and forgive my family role models as appropriate.

I now release and forgive the society role models as appropriate.

I now release and forgive the church role models as appropriate.

I now release and forgive the media role models as appropriate.

I now release and forgive the _____role models as appropriate.

I now release and forgive all modeling of what's expected of women/men.

I now transcend female/male role models.

Having a role model and I are one.

I now release and forgive my mother/father for being a role model.

I now release and forgive my mother/father for not being a role model.

I now release and forgive myself for having a role model.

I now release and forgive myself for not having a role model.

I now transcend having a role model.

Being a role model and I are one.

I now release and forgive myself for being a role model. .

I now release and forgive myself for not being a role model.

I now transcend being a role model.

The filling-the-cup script:

I am my own role model.

I role model success for myself, releasing all else.

I create my personal role model composite as appropriate.

I evaporate all else from my consciousness.

I visualize my future possibilities as limitless.

I am filled with miracle consciousness.

What others have done, I can do.

I have unique talents and I know it.

I am at peace with my unique talents and skills.

I am now willing to recognize and accept my purpose.

I am now willing to live my purpose.

My next step is clear to me now.

I transcend gender as a factor in my success.

I transcend race as a factor in my success.

I transcend age as a factor in my success.

I transcend _____ as a factor in my success.

My success has all positive outcomes for me now.
I am loved and accepted when I am successful.
I am supported and nurtured when I am successful.
I am safe and protected when I am successful.
I am happy and healthy when I am successful.
I am joyful and spontaneous when I am successful.
I am completely at peace with my success issues.
I take steps toward my increasing success daily.
I feel good about myself when I am successful.
I am success.

Success I: Female

The filling-the-cup script:
I deserve to be successful.
I deserve to be prosperous and wealthy.
I deserve to be healthy and happy.
I deserve to have everything in my life work now.
It is safe for me to stand out.
It is safe for me to excel.
It is safe for me to have unlimited success.
It is natural for me to have unlimited success.
It is appropriate for me to have unlimited success.
I have success consciousness now.
I dissolve all past conditioning as appropriate.
I maintain my uniqueness as I become increasingly
* successful.*
I have faith in my unlimited powers.
I use my unlimited power for global good.
I am now willing to have everything in my life.
I am now willing to have all of my relationships work.
I am now willing to have all of my business dealings work.
I am now willing to have all of my personal issues resolved.
I now choose to be fully conscious about my success issues.
I define success by my own terms.
I revel in my own success.
Individuality and I are one.
Inner strength and I are one.
Authority and I are one.
Integrity and I are one.
Uniqueness and I are one.
Self direction and I are one.
Leadership and I are one.
Mommy and I are one.
Daddy and I are one.
Being a woman has all positive outcomes for me now.
Being a successful woman has all positive outcomes for me
* now.*
I recognize and honor my own femininity and womanhood.
I am unique and distinct in my individual femininity and
* womanhood.*

231

I am unlimited in the definition and development of my femininity.

My path to success is my own.

My path to success is individual and unique.

The male model and my definition of success are separate for me now.

The male model and my path to success are separate for me now.

The male model and my definition of femininity are separate for me now.

I am at peace with my masculine side.

I am at peace with my feminine side.

My masculine side and my feminine side are in balance.

I now release all past issues around my femininity.

I am in control of my own identity process.

I set my own expectations for my definition of my femininity.

My inner ideas of femininity are mine and mine alone.

I am safe and protected when I define my femininity for myself.

I am loved and accepted when I define my femininity for myself.

I am successful when I define my womanhood for myself.

I face my womanhood rites of passage wise, free, and unafraid.

I face all emerging stages of my womanhood wise, free, and unafraid.

I accept my womanhood transitions with grace and power.

I accept my womanhood transitions with dignity and respect.

I honor myself for the woman I am now and the woman I am becoming.

I am powerful with my unique and individual womanhood.

I am at peace with my feminine power.

I am safe with my feminine power.

I am happy with my feminine power.

I use my power for global good.

I use my power for prosperity and abundance for all.

I use my power for increasing health and happiness.

I value myself and my power.

I honor myself and my power.

I acknowledge myself and my power.
My power enhances all of my relationships.
As I increase in power, all of my relationships increase in power.
My inner strength increases as I increase my power.
My inner peace increases as I increase my power.
My inner balance increases as I increase my power.
I acknowledge the power of man.
Manhood compliments my womanhood.
Manhood enhances my womanhood.
Manhood strengthens my womanhood.
Manhood embraces my womanhood.
My success increases as I increase my womanpower.
I deserve success.
I deserve prosperity and abundance.
I deserve love and pleasure.
I am safe when I am successful.
I am loved when I am successful.
I am nurtured when I am successful.
I am unique when I am successful.
I am normal when I am successful.
I am my own person when I am successful.
I experience joy and love when I am successful.
I am my own model of success.
Success and I are one.
Modeling success and I are one.
I am successful in who I am.
I am successful in what I do.
I provide value with who I am and what I do.
I provide value and receive value equally.
I am safe when I receive.
I am loved when I receive.
I am happy when I receive.
I am at peace when I receive.
Success and peace are one for me.
Completion and peace are one for me.
Closure and peace are one for me.
I complete my personal processing in all peaceful ways.
I recognize universal source as the source of all success.
I include higher purpose in all of my success dealings.

Higher purpose and I are one.
I circulate prosperity and abundance freely.
Abundance and prosperity flow through me effortlessly.
I am a part of the abundant whole.
Everything I do adds to the abundance of the whole.
I interact with abundance synergistically.
I accept all of the good the world holds.
I am safe with all of the good the world has to offer.
As a woman, I deserve to be realized.
As a woman, I am worthy of being realized.
As a woman, I am at peace with being realized.
I have arrived.
I am success.

Success I: Male

The filling-the-cup script:
I deserve to be successful.
I deserve to be prosperous and wealthy.
I deserve to be healthy and happy.
I deserve to have everything in my life work now.
It is safe for me to stand out.
It is safe for me to excel.
It is safe for me to have unlimited success.
It is natural for me to have unlimited success.
It is appropriate for me to have unlimited success.
I have success consciousness now.
I dissolve all past conditioning as appropriate.
I maintain my uniqueness as I expand myself.
I maintain my uniqueness as I expand my manhood.
I maintain my uniqueness as I become increasingly
   successful.
I have faith in my unlimited powers.
I use my unlimited power for global good.
I am now willing to have everything in my life.
I am now willing to have all of my relationships work.
I am now willing to have all of my business dealings work.
I am now willing to have all of my personal issues resolved.
I now choose to be fully conscious about my success issues.
I define success by my own terms.
I revel in my own success.
Individuality and I are one.
Inner strength and I are one.
Authority and I are one.
Integrity and I are one.
Uniqueness and I are one.
Self direction and I are one.
Leadership and I are one.
Mommy and I are one.
Daddy and I are one.
My father's manhood and I are one.
I recognize my father as the primary source of my manhood.
I honor my father's manhood.

I honor and recognize my own manhood.
I am unique and distinct in my individual manhood.
I am unlimited in my definition of manhood and manliness.
I am unlimited in my development of my manhood and manliness.
My path to manhood is my own.
My path to manhood is individual and unique.
I am at peace with my masculine side.
I am at peace with my feminine side.
My masculine side and my feminine side are in balance.
I now release all past issues around my masculinity.
I now release all past issues around my manhood.
My inner ideas of manhood are mine and mine alone.
I am in control of my own identity process.
I set my own expectations for my definition of my manhood.
I am safe and protected when I define my manhood for myself.
I am loved and accepted when I define my manhood for myself.
I am loyal when I define my manhood for myself.
I am successful when I define my manhood for myself.
I face my manhood rites of passage wise, free, and unafraid.
I face all emerging stages of my manhood wise, free, and unafraid.
I accept my manhood transitions with grace and power.
I accept my manhood transitions with dignity and respect.
I honor myself for the man I am now and the man I am becoming.
I am powerful with my unique and individual manhood.
I am at peace with my feminine power.
I am safe with my manpower.
I am happy with my manpower.
I use my manpower for global good.
I use my manpower for prosperity and abundance for all.
I use my manpower for increasing health and happiness.
I value myself and my manpower.
I honor myself and my manpower.
I acknowledge myself and my manpower.
Manhood and I are one.
Manpower and I are one.

My manpower has all positive outcomes for me now.
My manpower enhances all of my relationships.
*As I increase in manpower, all of my relationships increase
    in power.*
My inner strength increases as I increase my manpower.
My inner peace increases as I increase my manpower.
My inner balance increases as I increase my manpower.
I acknowledge the power of woman.
Womanhood compliments my manhood.
Womanhood enhances my manhood.
Womanhood strengthens my manhood.
Womanhood embraces my manhood.
My success increases as I increase my manpower.
I deserve success.
I deserve prosperity and abundance.
I deserve love and pleasure.
I am safe when I am successful.
I am loved when I am successful.
I am nurtured when I am successful.
I am unique when I am successful.
I am normal when I am successful.
I am my own person when I am successful.
I experience joy and love when I am successful.
I am my own model of success.
Success and I are one.
Modeling success and I are one.
I am successful in who I am.
I am successful in what I do.
I provide value with who I am and what I do.
I provide value and receive value equally.
I am safe when I receive.
I am loved when I receive.
I am happy when I receive.
I am at peace when I receive.
Success and peace are one for me.
Completion and peace are one for me.
Closure and peace are one for me.
I complete my personal processing in all peaceful ways.
I recognize universal source as the source of all success.
I include higher purpose in all of my success dealings.

Higher purpose and I are one.
I circulate prosperity and abundance freely.
Abundance and prosperity flow through me effortlessly.
I am a part of the abundant whole.
Everything I do adds to the abundance of the whole.
I interact with abundance synergistically.
I accept all of the good the world holds.
I am safe with all of the good the world has to offer.
As a man, I deserve to be realized.
As a man, I am worthy of being realized.
As a man, I am at peace with being realized.
I have arrived.
I am success.

Success II: Ambition

The emptying-the-cup script:

Ambition and I are one.
I now release and forgive _____ for having ambition.
I now release and forgive _____ for not having ambition.
I now release and forgive myself for having ambition.
I now release and forgive myself for not having ambition.
I now transcend ambition.
Living up to my potential and I are one.
I now release and forgive _____ for living up to his/her potential.
I now release and forgive _____ for not living up to his/her potential.
I now release and forgive myself for living up to my potential.
I now release and forgive myself for not living up to my potential.
I now transcend living up to my potential.
Pushing myself and I are one.
I now release and forgive _____ for pushing him/herself.
I now release and forgive _____ for not pushing him/herself.
I now release and forgive myself for pushing myself.
I now release and forgive myself for not pushing myself.
I now transcend pushing myself.
Competition and I are one.
I now release and forgive competition.
I now release and forgive _____ for being competitive.
I now release and forgive _____ for not being competitive.
I now release and forgive _____ for competing with me.
I now release and forgive myself for being competitive.
I now release and forgive myself for being competitive with _____.
I now release and forgive myself for not being competitive.
I now release and forgive myself for not being competitive with_____.
I now transcend competition.
Ruthlessness and I are one.
I now release and forgive _____for being ruthless.

I now release and forgive myself for being ruthless.
I now release and forgive myself for not being ruthless.
I now transcend ruthlessness.

The filling-the-cup script:

I am safe and protected when I am ambitious.
I am loved and nurtured when I am ambitious.
I have powerful and loving friends when I am ambitious.
I am feminine when I am ambitious (for women).
Ambition and the male model are separate for me now.
Ambition and money are separate for me.
Ambition and being tough are separate for me.
Ambition and being ruthless are separate for me.
Ambition and being masculine are separate for me now.
Ambition and being unethical are separate for me.
Ambition and being a hard driver are separate for me.
Ambition and _____are separate for me.
Ambition and personal satisfaction are the same for me.
Ambition and being happy are the same for me.
*Ambition and being balanced and healthy are the same
    for me.*
Ambition and taking care of myself are the same for me.
Ambition and getting what I want are the same for me.
*Ambition and working for the highest good are the same
    for me.*
Ambition and _____are the same for me.
I define ambition for myself.
I define ambition by my own standards.
It is natural and normal for me to be ambitious.
It is fun and exciting for me to be ambitious.
It is _____for me to be ambitious.
My ambition has all positive outcomes for me now.
I am at peace with myself and my ambition.

Success II: Business

The emptying-the-cup script:

Business prosperity and I are one.

I now release and forgive myself for being prosperous in business.

I now release and forgive myself for not being prosperous in business.

I now release and forgive _____ for not being prosperous in business.

Being like _____ and being prosperous in business are separate for me now.

I now transcend being prosperous in business.

Economic power and I are one.

I now release and forgive myself for having economic power.

I now release and forgive myself for not having economic power.

I now release and forgive ____ for not understanding economic power.

I release and forgive myself for not understanding economic power.

I now dissolve all family issues around economic power as appropriate.

I now dissolve all societal issues around economic power as appropriate.

I now dissolve all_____ issues around economic power as appropriate.

I now transcend economic power.

The filling-the-cup script:

I am a competent businessperson.

I understand the elements of business.

I continually learn more about economics.

I continually learn more about marketing.

I continually learn more about management.

I continually learn more about my field of business.

I stay on top of the business trends.

I read in various fields to keep my perspective.

My business perspective is accurate.

I see and analyze trends that affect me and my business.

My business mind is active.

My creative mind is active.

My business and creative mind form a wonderful partnership.

I recognize viable business opportunities easily.

I distinguish profitable ideas readily.

I have good business sense and judgment.

I am discriminating in the business directions I pursue.

I am objective when I analyze my own business.

I am a skilled financial forecaster for my business.

I provide value to the universe and am rewarded for my service.

I give and receive value equally.

I provide a valuable service by _____.

I enjoy planning for my business.

I enjoy marketing myself and my business.

I take responsibility for making my business a success.

I am filled with success consciousness.

My greatest pleasure is my source of financial success.

Abundance is the natural state of the economy.

Abundance is my natural state of being.

I flow easily with the economic trends.

I maintain sufficient cash flow to keep my business growing.

I make appropriate business decisions easily and effortlessly.

I focus on what works, eliminating anything else from my business.

I attract positive business opportunities to myself.

I attract prosperous business opportunities to myself.

I recognize the appropriate directions to take.

My creative mind creates my wealth.

I tithe in time and service to the community that supports me financially.

I am one with my business prosperity.

My business prosperity is me.

I have the innate ability to provide prosperity for myself and others.

I go for the win-win in business situations, and I prosper.

Test Taking

The emptying-the-cup script:
Taking tests and I are one.
I now release and forgive myself for being frightened by tests.
I now release and forgive myself for not being frightened by tests.
I now release and forgive myself for taking tests well.
I now release and forgive myself for not taking tests well.
I now release and forgive the school system for stressing tests over learning.
I now release and forgive _____ for scaring me with tests.
I now transcend taking tests.

The filling-the-cup script:
I enjoy taking tests.
Taking tests is fun for me.
I enjoy studying for tests.
I retain what I study easily.
I recall information that I have read effortlessly.
I remember information I have heard with ease.
I enjoy finding solutions to the problems.
I enjoy finding the right answers to the questions.
My mind flows effortlessly when I am taking a test.
I am always prepared completely.
It is fun for me to learn _____.
It is fun for me to study _____.
Questions about _____ are fun for me to answer.
I enjoy writing about _____.
I begin taking tests with enthusiasm.
I begin taking tests quickly and confidently.
I understand the directions quickly.
I get a sense of the complete test effortlessly.
I remain calm and relaxed as I begin working.
I see myself achieving competently.
I see myself completing each section on time.
I see myself well ahead of the time frames for the test.
My hand is loose and flexible throughout the test.

My breathing is deep and relaxed throughout the test.
I see myself halfway through the test, and I am relaxed.
I see myself halfway through the test, and I am refreshed.
I see myself halfway through the test, and I am confident.
My body maintains its normal temperature.
I am at ease.
I am physically relaxed and comfortable.
I am achieving well.
My path to success with this test is clear.
I continue to concentrate easily.
I continue to focus effortlessly.
My mental activity is clear and quick.
My mind makes connections quickly.
I see the correct answers with ease.
I answer confidently.
I move through the questions easily.
My thought processes are sharp and clear.
I see the last question. I am smiling.
I feel confident about my test taking abilities.
I know my material, and I show it.
I win again!

Time Management

The emptying-the-cup script:
Time management and I are one.
I now release and forgive myself for managing time well.
I now release and forgive myself for not managing my time well.
I release and forgive _____ for modeling poor time management to me.
I release and forgive _____ for being a good time manager.
I now transcend time management.

The filling-the-cup script:
I am in control of my time and my life.
I take full responsibility for how I spend my time.
I enjoy being responsible for my time.
I make daily "to do" lists.
I prioritize my to do lists into A's, B's, and C's.
I spend A time on my A's.
I spend B time on my B's.
I spend C time on my C's.
I plan my time based on my to do list.
I plan my time based on my priorities.
I'm in tune with my rhythms and I use them productively.
I work on my top priorities during my most productive periods of the day.
I follow my plan for my time.
I allow time each day for the unexpected.
I allow time each day for myself.
I plan time each day for thinking and reviewing.
I plan time regularly for brainstorming and being creative.
I am reasonable when I plan my time.
I plan my time carefully and I follow my plan.
Time is my friend and I use it well.
I am comfortable scheduling tasks and timelines.
I maintain my timelines with ease.
I begin projects in a timely manner.
I do one thing at a time.
I focus my attention on the task at hand.

I begin tasks early.
I complete tasks early.
I work in smooth steps toward completion.
I work in installments on projects.
I enjoy getting things done on time.
I meet deadlines easily.
It is easy and fun for me to be on time.
I use waiting time productively.
I carry my calendar with me at all times.
My calendar is always up to date.
I am well organized; I am efficient; I am flexible.
I am effective in planning my time and following my plan.
I take pleasure in having a smooth life.
I now release all past issues around time.
I now release all past issues around scheduling.
I now release all past issues around completion.
I now release all past issues around being on task.
I enjoy getting things done on time.
I get high naturally on getting things done on time.
I have enough time to complete all of my tasks effectively.
It's OK for me to get everything done easily and effortlessly.
I am now enjoying accomplishing things easily and
  effortlessly.
I am an effective manager of my time.
I invest my time wisely.
I have sufficient time to do everything I want.
I do the right things naturally.
I do the right things as appropriate.
I recognize effective action instantly and I take it.
My time and I are one.
Time and I work well together.
Time and I function as a smooth team.
My time and I make good partners.
I find excitement in having spare time for myself.
I spend quality time with myself.
I plan time alone.
I plan time for leisure regularly.
I am my time, and I use it well.

Transcendence

The emptying-the-cup script:
Releasing and I are one.
I am safe and protected when I release and let go.
The abundant universe provides for me when I release and let go.
I am now willing to empty myself.
I am now willing to empty myself emotionally.
I am now willing to empty myself mentally.
I am now willing to empty myself physically.
I am now willing to empty myself spiritually.
I am now willing to release perceptions and definitions.
I am now willing to release thought patterns.
I am now willing to release patterns and limits.
I am now willing to release the past.
I am now willing to release the present.
I am now willing to release the future.
I now transcend time and time frames.
I am now willing to release all roles.
I am now willing to release the old me.

The filling-the-cup script:
Transcendence and I are one.
I transcend easily and effortlessly.
I transcend in peace and harmony.
I move through each stage with ease and joy.
I now transcend my role as a woman/man.
I now transcend my role as a daughter/son.
I now transcend my role as a mother/father.
I now transcend my role as a wife/husband.
I now transcend my role as an enabler.
I now transcend my role as a lover.
I now transcend my role as a nurturer/provider.
I now transcend my role as a friend.
I now transcend my role as _____.
I now transcend my cultural background.
I now transcend my birthright and my roots.
I now transcend my family and my family patterns.

I now transcend my society and social rules.
I now transcend my conditioning and programming.
I now transcend winning and being first.
I now transcend surrendering.
I now transcend comfort and stability.
I now transcend commitment and consistency.
I now transcend loyalty.
I now transcend giving and receiving.
I now transcend loving and supporting.
*I now transcend recognizing, acknowledging, and
    empathizing.*
I now transcend polarities.
I now transcend balancing.
I now transcend control.
I now transcend having impact.
I now transcend my potential.
I now transcend my boundaries.
I now transcend my intelligence.
I now transcend my expectations of myself.
I now transcend my expectations of others.
I now transcend my expectation for outcomes.
I now transcend my profession/career.
I now transcend my measurements of success.
I now transcend my business and earning.
I now transcend my income.
I now transcend money, wealth, and materialism.
I now transcend risk.
I now transcend safety and security.
I now transcend my behavior.
I now transcend my personality.
I now transcend my responsibilities.
I now transcend my personal growth.
I now transcend my health and healing.
I now transcend the need to know.
I now transcend patterns and limits.
I now transcend thought patterns.
I now transcend _____.
I develop new structures daily.
I develop new models as appropriate.
I now incorporate the new models and structures with ease.

I now integrate the new models and structures in peace.
I now integrate polar opposites with ease.
I now integrate the whole in peace.
I create the new me effortlessly.
I fall in love with the new me daily.
I enjoy gaining new perspectives daily.
My ingenuous and spontaneous self is reborn daily.
I am at peace hanging out.
I am at peace hanging in.
I integrate my yin, yang, and ingenuous self.
I draw on universal source daily.
I set my new foundations as appropriate.
I move from pro-creation to world creation.
Creation and I are one.
Self creation and I are one.
Universal creation and I are one.
Transcendent creation and I are one.
I now transcend transcendence.

Winning Friends
and Influencing People

A filling-the-cup script:
I have a winning personality and it shows.
I am positive about myself and others.
I respect myself and I respect others.
I treat each person as an individual.
I treat each person as important.
I find something interesting in every person I meet.
I am genuinely interested in other people and it shows.
I like to learn more about the people in my life.
I enjoy the people in my life and it shows.
I appreciate the people in my life.
I encourage myself and others.
I arouse enthusiasm in myself and the people around me.
My voice radiates animation and enthusiasm.
I nourish my own self esteem.
I nourish the self esteem of others.
I support and nurture myself.
I support and nurture others.
I identify my own good points.
I identify the good points of others.
I recognize and praise the good points of others.
I show my gratitude openly and honestly.
I give honest and sincere appreciation to others.
I think about what the other person wants.
I see things from others' viewpoints.
I work for mutual gain in all I do.
I talk about others in positive ways.
I talk about others more than I talk about myself.
I have a heartwarming smile.
My smile shows through my voice.
I greet people with a smile.
I act happy: I whistle and sing.
I am cheerful.
I remember names and faces effortlessly.
I peg names and faces when I first meet them.
I recall a few facts about each person I meet.

I honor other's names, and I use their names often.
I am a good listener, and I listen intently.
My eyes are mild and genial.
I encourage others to talk with my voice, eyes, and body language.
I give my full attention to the person talking.
I give affirming body gestures to the person talking.
I make the other person feel important, and I do it sincerely.
I talk about what interests the other person.
I talk in terms of the other person's interests.
I find something to admire in everyone.
I pass on happiness.
I pass on honest admiration.
I do unto others as I would have them do unto me.
I recognize the true worth of the people in my life.
I say Thank You often, and I mean it sincerely.
I learn from every person I meet.
I talk to people about themselves.
I am diplomatic and tactful.
I use diplomacy and conciliation as appropriate.
I put disagreement in perspective.
I listen before I talk, and look for areas of agreement.
I am honest and tell the truth spontaneously.
I study others' viewpoints and ideas.
I show respect for others' opinions.
I am willing to understand others.
I thank others for their opinions when they differ from mine.
I think through our differences.
I am courteous at all times.
I am broad minded as appropriate.
Debating and feeling good are separate for me now.
Arguing and feeling good about myself are separate for me now.
Winning and being important are separate for me now.
Being right and feeling good are separate for me now.
I have the courage to admit my errors.
When I'm wrong, I admit it right away.
I say I am wrong quickly, openly, and with sincerity.
I talk about my own mistakes before I criticize others.

I always let the other person save face.
I ask questions instead of giving orders.
I praise the slightest improvement in others, and I mean it.
I give the other person a fine reputation to live up to.
I make any fault or mistake seem easy to correct.
I see myself objectively.
I see others objectively.
I realize we are all different, and I honor those differences.
I recognize the good of humankind.
I work for the good of humankind at all times.
I have an honest love of humankind.
It is appropriate to let my feelings for others show.
I am an optimist, and that is OK.
I am full of life, and I share my fullness openly and freely.
I use my people skills in all appropriate ways.
I use my people skills to improve myself and others.
I use my people skills to increase others' self worth.
I use my people skills to increase others' self esteem.
I provide value with who I am.
I provide value with what I do.
I am secure in my own value, and I share that openly.
I want to see others succeed, and I support them to succeed.
I work for the win-win at all times.
If I win, everybody wins: and if they win, I win.
I create peace and harmony in all my relationships.
I win friends easily and effortlessly.
I influence people in all appropriate ways.

(The ideas in this script were taken from *How to Win Friends and Influence People*, Dale Carnegie, Pocket Books, 1936.)

Wrestling

The emptying-the-cup script:
Wrestling and I are one.
I now release and forgive myself for wrestling to win.
I now release and forgive _____ for wanting me to win.
I now release and forgive myself for winning.
I now release and forgive myself for not winning.
I now transcend wrestling and winning.

The filling-the-cup script:
I enjoy wrestling.
Wrestling is fun for me.
I am good at wrestling.
I am completely relaxed and loose when I wrestle.
I concentrate on my opponent at all times.
I am always in good body position.
I am close to my opponent.
I have my weight over my legs.
My elbows are tight to my sides.
My hands are behind my knees in the proper position.
I maintain my proper body position.
I am close to my opponent.
I hear my opponent's breathing.
I hear my own breathing, which is deep and regular. .
All other sounds disappear.
I move toward my opponent.
I lower my altitude.
I jolt him hard.
I see myself running the pipeline successfully.
My forehead is in his stomach.
My hands are locked loosely on his leg.
I step quickly to my right.
I drop my hips and step straight back.
My head is up.
My hips are lower than my shoulders.
I feel the power of my body pressing down on his leg.
I see him hit the mat.
I attack instantly and break him down.

I'm in good body position.
My weight is over my legs.
I easily control his hips.
I move quickly to break him down.
I look for a pin situation.
I see his near arm pop up.
I bar it and start my pinning situation.
I've barred his arm.
I've trapped his far arm.
I start around his head.
I keep my weight down on my opponent.
I keep my weight into my opponent.
I am in good body position.
I maintain motion.
I feel my pressure and weight pushing him down.
My weight is all down on his shoulder and head.
I'm out in front now covering his head with my body.
He's on his back.
The official is looking for the pin.
The referee is slapping the mat.
I win.
I win again.
I love to wrestle.
I provide value to myself when I wrestle.
I provide value to my school when I wrestle.

Writing

The emptying-the-cup script:
Writing and I are one.
I now release and forgive myself for writing.
I now release and forgive myself for not writing.
I now transcend writing.

The filling-the-cup script:
It is fun to write and I enjoy writing.
I have a natural ability to express myself in writing.
I take pleasure putting my ideas on paper.
I feel satisfaction seeing my thoughts in print.
Simple, clear expression is natural to me.
I flow with ideas and ways to express them.
I gladly share my experiences.
I am good at putting ideas into words.
I have a natural flow with language.
I express myself clearly and simply.
I make writing schedules and I keep to my schedules.
I block out time for my writing regularly.
I maintain my writing time free and clear.
It is fun to make my deadlines.
I achieve within the appointed time easily and effortlessly.
My attention stays on task while I am writing.
I am motivated to write daily.
I create writing time easily and effortlessly.
I flow from the beginning to the end of my writing time.
I maintain my momentum through completion.
I love to edit my work.
I enjoy beginning new writing projects.
I enjoy completing existing writing projects.
My enthusiasm carries me through each project.
*I stay highly motivated from the beginning to the end of
   each project.*
I feel pleasure and pride when I write.
I feel natural and relaxed when I write.
I work well in any environment.
*I work well with any medium — typewriter, computer, tape
   recorder.*

I organize my materials quickly.
I focus my thoughts easily and effortlessly.
Characters spring to life for me.
My characters are real and they appear that way to others.
Dialogue flows for me.
My dialogue is real and appears that way to others.
Settings paint themselves for me.
My settings are real and they appear that way to others.
Appropriate details highlight themselves for me.
I am a tool in the writing process.
I present important messages in everyday stories.
Writing and I are one.
Dialogue and I are one.
Characters and I are one.
Settings and I are one.
Story lines and I are one.
Production and I are one.
I smile with pleasure as my work unfolds.
I trust my work to be good.
I am safe when I write.
I approve of my writing completely.
Others approve of my writing completely.
I enjoy being highly successful when I write.
My writing has all positive outcomes for me.
I am a talented writer.
I am an accomplished writer.
I am recognized nationally.
I am highly successful with my writing.
It brings me joy to be talented, creative, recognized, and
    successful.

How to order from

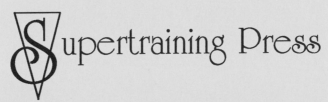

Supertraining Press

BY PHONE: Have your Visa or Mastercard ready and phone
(800) 762-9937

BY MAIL: Fill out the order form below and return it with your
check, money order, or credit card information to:

133

S

Supertraining Press
Box 10064
Sedona, AZ 86339

No. of copies   **Amount**

_____ copies of *Change Your Mind* - $19.95 + $3 postage   _____

_____ copies of *CYM Music Tape 1   2   3* (circle one) -
$19.95 + $1 postage for each tape   _____

Save by purchasing a book and music tape set:

_____ copies of *Change Your Mind and
Music Tape* 1   2   3 (circle one) - $35 + $4 postage   _____

                                              Total   _____

PAYMENT:

❑ **CHECK**   ❑ **VISA**   ❑ **MASTERCARD**

CARD # _____ **EXP. DATE** _____

SIGNATURE: _____

MAIL TO:
NAME: _____

ADDRESS: _____

CITY : _____

STATE, ZIP: _____

Thank you for your order.
Please allow 4 weeks for delivery.

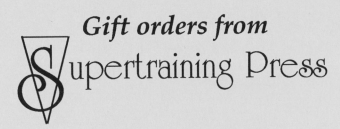

Gift orders from
Supertraining Press

BY PHONE: Have your Visa or Mastercard ready and phone
(800) 762-9937

BY MAIL: Fill out the order form below and return it with your check, money order, or credit card information to:

133
Sa

Supertraining Press
Box 10064
Sedona, AZ 86339

No. of copies	Amount
_____ copies of *Change Your Mind* - $19.95 + $3 postage	_____
_____ copies of *CYM Music Tape 1 2 3 (circle one)* - $19.95 + $1 postage for each tape	_____

Save by purchasing a book and music tape set:

_____ copies of *Change Your Mind and Music Tape 1 2 3 (circle one)* - $35 + $4 postage	_____
Total	_____

PAYMENT:

❏ CHECK   ❏ VISA   ❏ MASTERCARD

CARD # _____ EXP. DATE _____

SIGNATURE: _____

MAIL TO:
NAME: _____

ADDRESS: _____

CITY : _____

STATE, ZIP: _____

Gift card to read: _____

_____

_____

Thank you for your order.
Please allow 4 weeks for delivery.